THE KURDS

A
NATION
DENIED

Minority Rights Publications

Minority Rights Group is an international, non-governmental organization whose aims are to secure justice for minority (and non-dominant majority) groups suffering discrimination by:

1. Researching and publishing the facts as widely as possible to raise public knowledge and awareness of minority issues worldwide.

2. Advocating on all aspects of human rights of minorities to aid the prevention of dangerous and destructive conflicts.

3. Educating through its schools programme on issues relating to prejudice, discrimination and group conflicts.

If you would like to know more about the work of the Minority Rights Group, please contact Alan Phillips (Director), MRG, 379 Brixton Road, London SW9 7DE, United Kingdom.

m

Minority Rights Publications is a new series of books from the Minority Rights Group. Through the series, we aim to make available to a wide audience reliable data on, and objective analyses of, specific minority issues. The series draws on the expertise and authority built up by the Minority Rights Group over two decades of publishing. Further details on MRG's highly acclaimed series of reports can be found at the end of this book. Other titles in the book series are:

The Balkans: Minorities and States in Conflict
by Hugh Poulton (1991)

Armenia and Karabagh: The Struggle for Unity
Edited by Christopher J. Walker (1991)

The Kurds: A Nation Denied
by David McDowall

THE KURDS

A
NATION
DENIED

by
David McDowall

Foreword by
John Simpson

Minority Rights Publications

© Minority Rights Group 1992

First published in Great Britain
in 1992 by
Minority Rights Publications
379 Brixton Road
London SW9 7DE

British Library Cataloguing in Publication Data
A CIP catalogue record of this book is available from the British Library

ISBN 1 873194 15 3 paper
ISBN 1 873194 30 7 hardback

Library of Congress Cataloguing in Publication Data
CIP Data available from the Library of Congress

Designed and typeset by Brixton Graphics
Printed and bound by Billing and Sons Ltd

Cover photo of Kurdish Refugees after battle of Kirkuk, March 1991
Don McCullin/Magnum Photos Ltd

CONTENTS

FOREWORD

by John Simpson
BBC Foreign Affairs Editor

In March 1988, during the Iran-Iraq war, the Iranian air force flew a group of foreign journalists to a town in Iraqi Kurdistan which had just been taken over by a Kurdish guerrilla group and handed over to the advancing Iranian forces. The town was called Halabja, and most of us who were being taken there had never heard of it before. We were told that Iraq had counter-attacked with chemical weapons, and that 5000 people had died. Few of us, I suspect, thought it was more than the standard propaganda line.

When we reached Halabja we saw that, if anything, the figure was an underestimate. Bodies lay heaped up, ready for mass burial. Others lay where they had fallen when the bombs fell. Halabja stank of death and of one of the nastier forms of destruction. Saddam Hussein had responded in characteristic fashion to the Kurdish demand for an acknowledged political identity.

That demand has rarely received anything but a hostile and often violent rebuff. The skills of RAF Bomber Command were first learned in air raids on Kurdish villages in Iraq during the 1920s. Throughout the 20th century there have been punitive expeditions and attempts at forcible assimilation in many of the countries within whose borders the Kurdish people live.

In Turkey and the Arab countries the hostility to the Kurds is often racial in origin; but far more important is the unresolved question which the political identity of the Kurdish people poses for the successor states of the Ottoman Empire. The Treaty of S_rves in 1920 created the possibility of an independent Kurdish state, but events in Turkey and Britain's decision to include the Mosul area in the territory of the newly created state of Iraq soon ensured that it came to nothing.

Yet the Kurdish question, as David McDowall's book brings out, is a complex one. The Kurds themselves have usually been divided about their future. Iraq, which is a leading oppressor of the Kurds, has nevertheless long accepted their right to express their political and cultural identity in a way that Turkey, for instance, has never permitted. Before his conflict with the United Nations, Saddam Hussein would often pay heavily stage-managed visits to Kurdistan, dressed for the cameras in Kurdish costume. Across the border in Turkey, the law forbids the wearing of Kurdish national dress. Iraq gave a form of autonomy to its Kurds, though it was regulated fiercely by the army and the secret police; in Turkey, by contrast, the official term used to describe the Kurdish population is 'mountain Turks'. The only constant factor in the Kurdish experience is the inability to achieve the promise held out to them at Sèvres, seven decades ago.

For a brief moment in March 1991 the Kurds of northern Iraq experienced the exhilaration of controlling their own territory in freedom. It was quickly over. The United States and its allies, nervous that Iraq might fall apart as a unitary state, did nothing to prevent troops loyal to Saddam Hussein from recapturing large parts of Iraqi Kurdistan. For the Kurdish political parties, the old question – whether to enter into agreements with their enemies, and so run the risk of being divided and ruled – arose again.

In different forms and in different places, the question will never go away. David McDowall's well-informed book, thoughtful and unexcitable in the best tradition of Minority Rights Group publications is subtitled 'A nation denied'. It is a telling study of the cruelty and instability which arises when the claims of nationhood are ignored.

John Simpson

John Simpson joined the BBC in 1966 and has worked in Brussels, South Africa, as presenter of BBC Television *Nine O'Clock News* and is now the BBC's Foreign Affairs Editor. In 1990 he joined the BBC Newsnight team and in 1991 was named (joint) World Television Journalist of the Year for his reports from Baghdad during the Gulf War.

Acknowledgements

Most of this book has been previously published as *The Kurds*, MRG Report, 1989, but the whole has been revised, extended and updated to cover events until July 1991. Chapter 8 on the Alevi Kurds was previously published as *The Alevi Kurds: A Briefing on Alevi Kurd Asylumseekers*, a MRG Occasional Paper, in July 1989. David McDowall is the sole author of the work and the opinions expressed are his own.

Transliteration is always a problem, particularly in the case of the Kurds, where there are Kurdish, Arabic, Turkish and Persian words in use. As a result, consistency is not possible and the author has used spellings in common usage and transliterations commonly used in academic publications.

MRG gratefully thanks John Simpson for writing the Foreword to this book.

This book was produced by Kaye Stearman (Series Editor), Brian Morrison (Production Co-ordinator), Gloria Mitchell (Editorial Assistant), Robert Webb (Publicity and Marketing Co-ordinator).

About the author

David McDowall is a freelance writer and specialist on the Middle East. He is the author of MRG's reports *The Kurds, Lebanon: a Nation of Minorities* and *The Palestinians*, and *Palestine and Israel: The Uprising and Beyond* (I.B. Tauris, 1989).

Glossary of terms

Agha – chief or landlord

Ahl al Haqq – literally 'People of the Truth', also called *Ali-Ilahi*, Islamic sect, regarded by many Muslims as heretical

Alevis – Islamic sect, regarded by many Muslims as heretical

Beduin – Arabic nomads or transhumants

Doguculuk – literally 'Eastism', Kurdish movement advocating development of Eastern Turkey

Emir (or *Amir*) – prince, ruler

Emirates – principalities

Gurani – Kurdish sub-dialect, used in parts of Iran

Imam – Islamic religious leader

Jash – Kurdish irregular Iraqi-government militias

Kirmanshahi – Kurdish sub-dialect, used in parts of Iran

Kurmanji – one of two major Kurdish dialects, spoken from Mosul into USSR

Leki – Kurdish sub-dialect, used in parts of Iran

Majlis – 'council', either informal gathering or a formal chamber or assembly.

Naqshbandiya – dervish order

Qadiriya – dervish order

Qazi – judge

Pasdaran – Iranian Islamic Republic Revolutionary Guards

Pesh mergas – literally 'those who face death', Kurdish nationalist fighters *Sayyid* – a person descended from the Prophet Mohammed

Shaikh – Islamic religious leader

Sorani – one of two major Kurdish dialects, spoken from Urmiya in the north to Khanaqin in the south; official Kurdish dialect used in Iraq

Turkkurtleri – literally 'true Turks', Turkish nationalist ideology

Umma – Islamic religious community

Vilayet – province, of the Ottoman Empire

Yazidism – syncretic religion, followed by a small number of Kurds

Zaza – Kurdish sub-dialect, spoken in parts of Anatolia

INTRODUCTION

The mass flight of Kurds from Iraq in April 1991 brought world attention to the Kurdish question as no previous event had done. Many people learnt, for the very first time, of this large Middle Eastern community. Media reporting, which concentrated on the scale of the tragedy, inevitably created simple images of the Kurds – as perennial victims of oppressive and wicked governments, and as a nation which had somehow been betrayed.

No one can doubt that the Kurdish people have been victims rather than determinants of the regional political developments during the 20th Century. Nor can one doubt that the Kurds have already travelled a long way in the process of national formation. Yet to describe the Kurds simply as victims runs the risk of demeaning them, of stripping them of responsibility for their own actions.

To describe the Kurds as a 'nation', as people in Western Europe understand a nation, risks ignoring the complex and sometimes difficult relationship many Middle Eastern communities have with the idea of 'nation' as Europeans define it. Yet the subtitle of this book, *A Nation Denied*, is intended to signal the central challenge faced by the Kurdish people: the forging of a national identity despite outside opposition and, possibly more surprisingly, despite the contradictions within Kurdish society itself.

Many Middle Eastern communities have travelled down a difficult path in nation-building, some successfully, others less so. Most Middle Eastern historians would probably consider the invasion of European thought into the body politic of Middle Eastern society in the second half of the 19th Century as the main source of this sense of national identity. This invasion reached its most dramatic stage in the collapse of the Ottoman Empire in World War I, and the struggle of the many communities within that empire to find a new identity which could conform to the new world order imposed by the West. Amongst the many communities engaged in that search – the Greeks and other Balkan peoples, the Arabs, the Turks, the Jews and the Armenians – were also the Kurds. Most of these communities claimed an almost

1

divine right to nationhood, in at least one case within God-given borders.

In the case of the Armenians and Kurds, the borders of their respective homelands overlapped to a very great extent indeed. Had it not been for the liquidation of the Armenian community in Anatolia in waves of massacre and deportation from 1896 through to 1922 (in which the Kurds participated), the Kurds and Armenians might have had to forge a new concept of 'nation' embracing both communities. Or there might have been genocidal war, or partition involving the immense and forced migration of thousands, if not millions, of Armenians and Kurds into their appropriate 'nation-state'.

These things did not happen because the Armenians as a community in Turkey had ceased to exist. But it is worth remembering that the concept of nation-state, as founded upon religious, linguistic or racial difference, is a powerful form of exclusivity. Indeed, it could be said that many Armenians perished because of it, at the hands of the Turks who were themselves determining their national identity. Imposed upon the ruins of a multiracial and multi-confessional empire, where people of different belief, custom and ethnicity had lived side by side in both town and country throughout most of both the Ottoman and the Persian Empires, this virulent exclusivity has had a devastating effect on Middle East civilization.

The Turks, the Jews, the Arabs and the Balkan peoples were successful in establishing national states (though in the Jewish case this was achieved not by Ottoman subjects but by European colonists, and at the expense of the indigenous inhabitants). The Kurds were unsuccessful. However, not one of the nation-states that have emerged in the area, not even Israel, which many might think most closely approximates to a real (ie. European) nation-state, has fully resolved the problem of national identity and reconciled its communities to it.

In a memorandum to his government in the early 1930s, Faisal, the first king of Iraq, summed up not only his own country's current (and continuing) problems of identity, but those (though the players might be different) of Iraq's neighbours:

'This government rules over a Kurdish group most of which is ignorant and which includes persons with personal ambitions who call upon this group to abandon government because it is not of their race. [It also] rules a Shi'a plurality which belongs to the same ethnic group as the government. But as a result of the discriminations which the Shi'is incurred under Ottoman rule which did not allow them to participate in the affairs of government, a wide breach developed between these two

sects. Unfortunately, all of this led the Shi'is... to abandon a govern-
ment which they consider to be very bad... I discussed these great mass-
es of the people without mentioning the other minorities, including
Christian, which were encouraged to demand different rights. There are
also other huge blocks of tribes... who want to reject everything related
to government because of their interests and the ambitions of their
shaikhs, whose powers recede if a government exists... I say with my
heart full of sadness that there is not yet in Iraq an Iraqi people.[11]

What is it that persuades Kurds they are one people? They do not, in
all probability, belong to a single ethnic origin but to an amalgam.
They do not enjoy a distinctive religion, for most of them, perhaps
85%, follow Sunni Islam, although their adherence to a number of religious orders distinguishes the loyalties of different Kurdish villages.
Nor do the Kurds yet enjoy a unified language. One group of Kurds still
has difficulty understanding another. Moreover, as the relatively recent
history of the Kurds shows, they are torn apart by internal quarrels and
disputes, many of them rooted not in the ideology of liberation, but in
more ancient rivalries.

Nevertheless the Kurds continue to claim that by race, language, and
lifestyle – and perhaps above all by geography – they form a distinct
community. Put quite simply, they are more like each other than any-
body else and they feel it.

The vast majority still live in a mountainous region, concentrated
today between the Turks, Iraqi Arabs and Iranians. The governments of
Turkey, Iraq and Iran, which have difficulty agreeing on a number of
regional issues, are utterly agreed on one point: not one of them views
with any favour at all a separate Kurdish state in their midst. With the
present exception of Iraq, they view with profound disquiet any form
of autonomy, since this is suspect as a stepping stone to self-determination.

As aspirant nation-states themselves, with their own ideology
grounded in race (Turkey), or in the case of Iran in Shi'i Islam, and in
defined borders, they understand very well the dangers of allowing too
much head to Kurdish national feeling. It is as easy to see why they
should feel thus as it is to see the strength of the Kurdish case. Strategic
security, historical experience, the difficulties already experienced with
their neighbours, and the vital question of unexploited minerals leave
the Kurdish case for independent nation status as unnegotiable as its
justice may seem unanswerable.

Smaller Kurdish communities exist in Syria, Lebanon and USSR, as
well as urban communities in the larger cities of the region, Ankara

and Istanbul, Tehran and Tabriz, Mosul and Baghdad, Damascus and Beirut.

It is easy to assume that the difficult relationship between the Kurds and their neighbours results solely from nationalism and the question of self-determination. However, trouble between the Kurds and their neighbours has been intermittent virtually since the beginning of history, an expression of the long-standing tension between people of the hills and those of the plains.

From time immemorial, the inaccessible but habitable areas of the Middle East, the deserts, mountains and marshes, have been a refuge for those whose way of life is different from those who populate the cultivable plains. This 'Land of Insolence'[2], comprising the zones beyond the reach of government, has always been in a state of flux. Part of this land, the desert and the marshes, has now surrendered to the government of urban man, even though as late as 1991 the Tigris-Euphrates marshes were used as a refuge by Shi'i Arabs fleeing Saddam Hussein. In the hills of the Middle East, the Land of Insolence continues to flourish, from the religiously distinct communities of Lebanon, the Maronites and the Druzes, which periodically exert their independence from government, to Afghanistan, where tribespeople have found new reasons for repudiating the government of the plain.

It would be a mistake to conclude that such people, with their fierce independence of spirit, their pride in a distinctive culture, their corresponding disdain for the ways of the plainspeople, and their resistance to the encroachment of government, want nothing from the cities and people of the plains. Despite the tensions of the relationship they all, to a greater or lesser extent, live in a relationship of interdependence with the plain, and the distinction between two cultures can be more apparent than real. Indeed, it could be said that the outbreaks of conflict between the Kurds and their neighbours, like those between beduin and settled folk, occurred when something disturbed the delicate arrangements evolved for coexistence.

It is easy to portray the Kurdish question as essentially a conflict between a liberation movement and its repressive neighbours. The truth is a good deal more complex, not least because like other mountain people the Kurdish people wrestle between the strength of their long-standing and traditional identity, and the weakness of political development. In his remarkable study, Martin van Bruinessen puts his finger on a singular feature:

'*The Kurdish movement (in Iraq) had, especially since 1966, a conservative, even reactionary appearance, in spite of the justice of its*

4

demands. The Kurdish leadership seemed to wish for more imperialist interference in the region rather than less... the movement was gradually purged of its leftist elements and it seemed that the traditional leaders, whose authority had at first been challenged by young urban nationalists. were able to consolidate or recuperate their positions as a consequence of their participation in the movement.[3]

There is an obvious external reason for the apparently traditional nature of the Kurdish movement in the Soviet patronage of the Iraqis at that time, and the willing support of the Kurds by Imperial Iran and the United States. However, there were equally strong internal reasons for Kurdish conservatism, based on primordial loyalties, on social organization, on the interplay between tribe and state rooted in long-standing Kurdish experience, and the harsh fact that nationalism in rural areas could only operate through traditional channels. 'Kurdish nationalism and tribal and religious loyalties stand in ambivalent relationship to each other',[4] and it is reasonable to ask whether the traditionalist leaders, even as late as the 1970s, were really as interested in tribal autonomy, as were their forebears, as in the constitutional autonomy for which they publicly called.

The internal conflicts which have characterized Kurdish revolts inevitably raise the question whether the worst enemies of Kurdish national aspirations are the governments that have so brutally oppressed the Kurds over the past 60 years, or whether almost as great an impediment has been less visible, the fragmentary nature of Kurdish society and the less than national aspirations of many of its more traditionally minded people.

The purpose of this book therefore is to explore the identity of the Kurds, their bonds of loyalty, and their historical and recent experience since the break-up of the Ottoman Empire, to look at their position in the different countries in which they find themselves, and to pinpoint some of the internal and external factors and contradictions which exist today that both motivate and impede Kurdish nationalism.

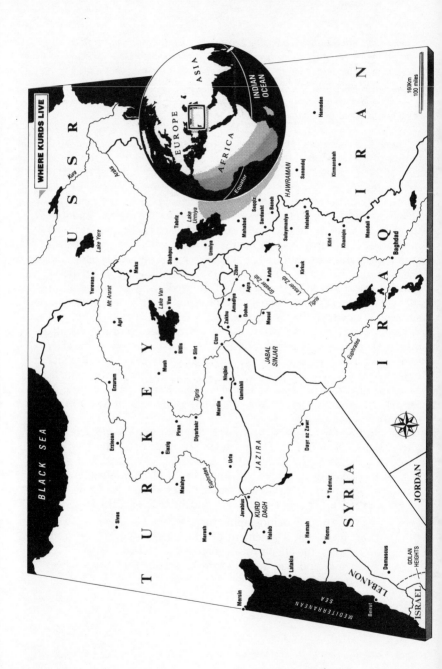

1

Kurdistan –
THE LAND OF THE KURDS

The land

Although Kurds are to be found in Syria, Soviet Armenia, Khorasan (in eastern Iran), and in Lebanon, the main concentration lives today where the Kurdish people have always lived, in the mountains where Iraq, Iran and Turkey meet. The heart of this area consists of the extremely rugged mountains of the Zagros range, running in ridges north-west to south-east. In the west these mountain folds give way to rolling hills falling to the Mesopotamian plain. To the north the mountains slowly turn to the steppe-like plateau and highlands of what used to be known as Armenian Anatolia.

Although the population is not exclusively Kurdish in much of this area, the dominant culture is Kurdish. Since the early 13th Century much of this area has been called Kurdistan, although it was not until the 16th Century, after the Kurds had moved north and west onto the Anatolian plateau by a series of tribal migrations, that the term Kurdistan came into common usage to denote a system of Kurdish fiefs. Since that time, although the term Kurdistan appears on few maps, it is clearly more than a geographical term since it refers also to a human culture which exists in that land. To this extent Kurdistan is a social and political concept.

Nevertheless no map of Kurdistan can be drawn without contention, and for this reason the demographic map, *Where Kurds Live*, is not a political statement, but a statement of where large numbers of Kurds are found. Turkey for all practical purposes denies Kurdistan's existence, whilst Iran and Iraq are reluctant to acknowledge that it is as extensive as many Kurds would have them accept.

Nowhere is this dispute more sharply demonstrated than in the quarrel over Kirkuk, on account of its vast oilfield. Is it Kurd or is it Arab? The Kurds claim it as Kurdish. The Iraqi government would reply that it is Iraqi. At the turn of the century, however, Kirkuk was predominantly Turkoman, though Turkish, Arabic, and Kurdish were spo-ken by those resident in Kirkuk. To its south and west were nomad Arabs, and to its east the country of the Hamavand Kurds. The Turkomans, yet another regional minority, were and remain long-resi-dent descendants of Turkic tribes which moved into the area some centuries ago.

The more extravagant Kurdish claims include both Luristan (the southern part of the Zagros range) and the Syrian-Turkish border area across to the north-east corner of the Mediterranean (thereby giving the putative Kurdish state a convenient sea outlet).[5] One of the prime difficulties of the claim to any delineable limits, of course, lies in the extensive intermediate zones around the Kurdish heartlands, where Arab, Turk, Azeri, and Farsi co-exist with Kurds. In the villages around Arbil, an almost exclusively Kurdish city east of Mosul, for example, Arabs are in a considerable majority.

Within the mountain heartlands, the northern Zagros range, and the eastern Taurus there have lived other communities over the cen-turies: sizeable Christian communities, not only Armenian but also Assyrian (both Nestorian and Chaldean), Jewish communities, and Turks. At times these have also been viewed by outsiders as Kurdish, and certainly they (with the partial exception of the Armenians) belonged to a Kurdish mountain culture in the broader sense of the word. From Kermanshah southwards live the Lurs and Bakhtiars, tribespeople similar to the Kurds, and whom some Kurds claim to belong to the Kurdish nation, but who mostly do not claim this identi-ty themselves. To the east and north-east, Kurdish-populated areas give way to the Azeri Turk- populated plains of Azerbaijan. To the west, Kurdish villages overlap with Arab and Turkish ones towards the Tigris, and here many Kurds belong as much or more to the culture of the plain as they do to that of the mountain. In the north, Kurds and Turks merge together with a less easily discernible divide between the two, and perhaps here it is not possible to talk of two different geo-graphic cultures.

In the understated words of a Foreign Office Handbook written in 1919: 'the climate of these mountains is bracing all the year round'.[6] In the higher and more remote areas, the climate is intolerably hot and arid in summer and bitterly cold in winter. During the winter, from December to February, many mountain villages are entirely isolated. These remote areas are sparsely populated by pastoralists who spend the summer months in search of upland pastures, and pass the winters in the valley. Permanent settlement is confined to the riverine valleys, where the climate is less severe, and where water-borne silt allows cultivation. Even on the Anatolian plateau temperatures can be punishing. At the northern extremity of the Kurdish-populated area the mean January temperature is -13°C, whilst even to the south-west in Diyarbekir, the largest Kurdish city in Turkey, the mean January temperature is -0.5°C, yet by mid-August the people live with a mean temperature of 30°C. Even spring and autumn are subject to sudden alternation of hot and cold spells. There can be snowfalls as late as May.

A century ago Kurdistan provided the great oak beams for many houses in Mosul, and some were also floated downstream for the houses of Baghdad and Basra. Today one will look in vain for sufficient trees for such a trade. Oak galls, still used, sustained a trade for ink and for leather tanning. Apart from the few trees still standing, the majority are little more than scrub oak and other stunted trees. The old forests have gone, partly through increased demand for wood from the plain, partly by defoliation in modern war, but more devastatingly for firewood, and because of the depredations of the goats which kill shrubs and saplings. Reforestation is highly desirable not only to replenish wood stocks, but to halt serious erosion, and allow for greater moisture retention by the soil.

All Kurdish communities are assiduous stockbreeders, mainly of sheep, goats and some cattle, and on the Anatolian plateau there are a few areas where the Kurds still pursue semi-nomadic pastoralism. In all parts of Kurdistan the cultivation of cereals is important, accounting for roughly 15% of the total in Turkey, and 35% and 30% respectively in Iran and Iraq, although in the mountain valleys of the Zagros range it is only for local consumption. Elsewhere it is an income earner. The principal cash crop of the Kurdish foothills is tobacco, but it is of moderate quality and cannot compete in outside markets. Cotton is also grown, particularly in Anatolia. In the mountains fruit and vegetables are the main crops for local consumption. Not more than a third of Kurdistan's arable land is actually cultivated, of which one third is always fallow. The potential therefore is considerable.

The major mineral in Kurdistan is oil, found in commercial quantities in Kirkuk and Khanaqin (Iraq), Batman and Silvan in Turkey, and at Rumeylan in Syria. The exploitation of these oilfields by the respective governments heightens both the Kurdish sense of injustice and also governmental determination to allow no separatism to threaten these important resources. Other minerals in significant quantities include chrome, copper, iron, coal and lignite.

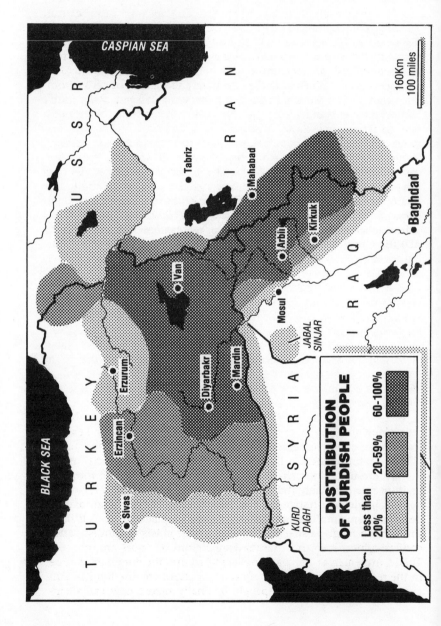

The people

The origin of the Kurdish people is uncertain. They have retained their distinct identity for at least two thousand years whilst their neighbours on the plains have suffered successive invasions and absorbed both foreign peoples and foreign cultures.

However it is unlikely that they are purely aboriginal, or derive from one single source. Most of them are probably the descendants of Indo-European tribes settling amongst aboriginal inhabitants in the mountains as much as four thousand years ago. Supposedly they were the mountain people in conflict with the Mesopotamian empires of Sumer, Babylon and Assyria, and the Kurds themselves believe they are descended from the Medes, although the linguistic evidence does not bear this out. Almost certainly these were amongst the Karduchoi (Kardu or Gutu) who gave Xenophon's Ten Thousand such a mauling during their famous retreat to the Black Sea in 400 BC.

Be that as it may, by the beginning of the Arab period (7th Century AD) the ethnic term 'Kurd' was applied to an amalgam of Iranian or Iranicized tribes, some autochthonous (possibly Kardu?), some semitic, and, probably, some Armenian communities.

As with the Arabs, the question of identity is not only to do with real ethnic origin. It is also to do with imagined lineage.[7] Religious fervour, among the Sunnis in particular, is inseparable from great respect for Arabic language and lineage, with which:

> *'the border Kurd almost invariably evinces a desire to identify himself...*
> *So we see [the tribal groups of] Hamavend, Baban, Shuan, and Jaf, all*
> *claiming Arab descent for their leaders, while yet very proud of being*
> *Kurds today.'*[8]

It is not surprising that *shaikhly* (religious) and other noble families frequently claim descent from the Prophet; those of such descent being able to claim the title *sayyid*.

Arab lineage is not all imagined. Some in relationship with the plainspeople inevitably did mingle Kurd with semitic ancestry, and it confers immense prestige on the putative descendant. And, as will become clear, Arab descent had a very special practical role for both the Kurdish religious shaikhs and also for the chiefs of Kurdish tribal confederations. It is also true that some 'Kurdish' tribes are probably Turkic, Armenian or Assyrian ones absorbed into the dominant culture in the region. Around Arbil, and no doubt elsewhere, the Kurdish language displaced others and people originally mixed now call themselves Kurds. More significant than ethnic purity, however, this society referred to as Kurdish developed its own distinctive culture which, despite the many internal differences from region to region and from tribe to tribe, contrasted with the cultures surrounding it, and established its own sense of identity.

How many Kurds?

Nothing, apart from the actual 'borders' of Kurdistan, generates as much heat in the Kurdish question as the estimate of the Kurdish population. Kurdish nationalists are tempted to exaggerate it, and governments of the region to minimize it. In Turkey only those Kurds who do not speak Turkish are officially counted for census purposes as Kurds, yielding a very low figure. On the other hand some enthusiasts have been tempted to assume that over 30% of Iraq is Kurdish, probably 7% in excess of the actual figure. Trying to estimate the current number of Kurds is not a very fruitful exercise, since no figures can be proven correct. The author is responsible for the figures below:[9]

Population estimates (1991)*

country	total population	Kurds	%
Turkey	57,000,000	10,800,000	19%
Iraq	18,000,000	4,100,000	23%
Iran	55,000,000	5,500,000	10%
Syria	12,500,000	1,000,000	8%
USSR	500,000		
Elsewhere	700,000		
Total		**22,600,000**	

*Estimates in rounded figures

Their language

Unlike the Arabs, the Kurds have not yet evolved a single systematized written or spoken language. To this day the Kurds are divided into dialect groups which cannot communicate freely with other Kurds in their mother tongue, although the majority share a north-western Iranian linguistic origin. In some cases limited comprehension is possible, elsewhere it is not. Some Kurds, of course, are able to speak more than one dialect, and the use of radio and printed material, and the

12

unifying effect of education are bound to improve the ease of communication considerably, and may even produce an eventual 'literary' style for broadcast and writing. The language is composed of two major dialects, but with considerable localized variations, and a number of sub-dialects:

Kurmanji, spoken northwards from Mosul into USSR. There are two literary forms, one using cyrillic characters (in USSR), the other using Hawar (Turcized Latin) characters (in Turkey);

Sorani (or **Kurdi**) which is spoken in a wide band across the international frontier from roughly Urmiya in the north to Khanaqin in the south. In Iraq this has become official Kurdish, indicating the cultural pre-eminence of Sulaymaniya over other Iraqi Kurd population centres. It is the only Kurdish language taught in schools or used by government.

Sub-dialects include **Kirmanshahi**, **Leki** and **Gurani**, spoken in the area of Iranian Kurdistan running from Kermanshah to Sanandaj, and **Zaza**, which is spoken in Dersim, an area of Anatolia inside an inverted triangle marked by Diyarbekir, Sivas and Erzerum. Although spoken at the opposite extremities of Kurdistan, Zaza and Gurani are closely related.

Their religion

Unlike the mountain peoples of Lebanon and Syria, the Druzes, Alawites and Isma'ilis and Christian Maronites, who declared their distinct identity through religious separatism from orthodoxy, the Kurds embraced Islam following the Arab conquests of the 7th Century AD. Previously tree and solar cults, Zoroastrianism, Judaism and Christianity had competed in the region. Religious *belief* plays no part in Kurdish distinctiveness.

Almost all the Kurds adhere to the **Shafi'i** school of law, one of the four established schools of **Sunni Islamic** jurisprudence, a mild distinction from their Sunni neighbours, the Turks, who mostly adhere to the Hanafi school. To the east the Azeri Turks, Persians and Lurs of Iran are all Shi'is. Religious difference is expressed *in practice*, with the widespread phenomenon of adherence to religious brotherhoods, particularly the **Qadiriya** and **Naqshbandiya**, and wild and eccentric manifestations of devotion.

Not all the Kurds adhere to Sunni Islam. In north-west Anatolian Kurdistan some Kurds adhere to an unorthodox form of Shi'ism, and are called **Alevis** (not to be confused with the Alawites of Syria), and are mainly Zaza-speaking (though neither all Zaza speakers are Alevis, nor are all Alevis Kurds; more are probably Turks). And in south-eastern and extreme south Kurdistan, in Kermanshah and Khanaqin provinces several Kurdish tribes subscribe to **Ithna'asheri Shi'i Islam**, the 'established' faith of Iran, thus demonstrating again that in religious matters Kurds have tended to conform with orthodoxy rather than declare their difference from it.

Two other religions, both considered 'Islamic deviations' exist amongst the Kurds:

Ahl al Haqq (People of the Truth), a small sect to be found in south and south-eastern Kurdistan. It is probably an extreme Shi'i syncretist deviation. They are also called the **Ali-Ilahi**, misleadingly since Ali (the Prophet Mohammed's son-in-law) is not the principal figure in their religious system. Their central belief is in seven successive manifestations of the Divinity, and they have in common with the Druzes and Alawis a veneration for Ali, though he is far outshadowed by the founder of their religion and the fourth 'theophany', the divinity, Shaikh or Sultan Sahak, who ushered in the fourth divine epoch, of **Haqiqa**, the 'Real Truth'.

Yazidism, another synthetic religion which has absorbed elements from almost every religion in the region including pagan, Zoroastrian (echoes of Persian dualism), Manichean (the Persian gnosis), Jewish (prohibition of certain foods), Nestorian Christian (baptism, drinking of wine, eucharistic rites) and Muslim (fasting, sacrifice, pilgrimage) elements and Isma'ili and Sufi beliefs (esoteric doctrine, ecstasy and reverence for a large number of initiate shaikhs), and Sabaean and Shamanistic features. They are to be found in USSR and also in Jabal Sinjar, due west of Mosul, although there are a small number and also their most sacred shrine in Shaikhan, due east of Mosul, and a few in Syria. During the 1830s and 1840s the Yazidis (and Christians) endured considerable persecution at the hands of their Muslim neighbours, Turk, Kurd and Arab, at various times, and many emigrated to the Caucasus. They are also found in the district of Diyarbekir, around Aintab (north of Aleppo), and some in Iran.

Yazidis probably do not exceed 100,000 today. They continue to be a persecuted community, although the allegation that they are devil-worshippers and many other things besides do not bear scrutiny.[10] The Yazidis are all Kurds, though they have frequently found common cause with Christian communities, largely on account of shared persecution. Since the 1950s, however, they have increasingly identified with Kurdish nationalism, partly on account of the discrimination suffered at governmental hands. In 1974 many Yazidis joined the Kurdish rebellion, and Yazidi leaders took refuge with the Barzanis that year.

Christians and Jews have always lived amongst the Kurds. As a result of the collapse of the old pluralism, political uncertainty and some persecution, there are now far fewer, though both are still to be found in the region:

Suriani (Syrian Orthodox) Christians in Tur Abdin near Mardin, and in Jazirah;

Assyrians, both Nestorian and Chaldean (erstwhile Nestorians now uniate with Rome) in Hakkari, Bahdinan, across to Urmiya;

and **Armenians** to the north, from Van northwards.

Most **Jews** did not leave until the 1950s, fearful of the bitter feelings created by the establishment of Israel in Arab Palestine.

It is interesting to note that Jews and Christians used to speak an almost identical ancient semitic dialect. Members of both faiths have lived in some places in separate villages and elsewhere mingled with Kurdish Muslims, providing a number of artisan skills which virtually disappeared once the majority of them left.

2

THE BASIS OF KURDISH SOCIETY – TRIBES, SHAIKHS AND AGHAS[11]

Kurdish society is essentially tribal, and derives from the largely nomadic and semi-nomadic existence of most Kurdish tribes in previous centuries. Loyalties, first to the immediate family, thence to the tribe, are quite as strong as in the Arab world. However, unlike the Arabs, Kurdish tribal cohesion is based on a mix of blood tie and territorial loyalty, and it should be remembered that a substantial number of Kurds in low-lying areas are not tribal even in a territorial sense. Nomadism, undoubtedly one source of tribal structure, rapidly diminished during the second half of the 19th Century and is now virtually nonexistent.

The bonds of religion

Alongside these tribal ties are strong religious loyalties, especially to the shaikhs, the local leaders of religious brotherhoods. This phenomenon is a good deal more recent, dating from the first half of the 19th Century, when two orders, the Qadiriya and the Naqshbandiya, began to spread very rapidly throughout Kurdistan. The reason for the success of these orders is discussed in Chapter 3.

The religious path was open to everyone. Through personal spiritual authority and through acquisition of land rights, even the poorest, given he was also ambitious, could reach the top of the social ladder as a landed shaikh. If his son chose to follow the path of religious study, a shaikhly dynasty imbued with temporal as well as religious power could be established. Mahmud Barzinja, Mulla Mustafa Barzani and Jalal Talabani (leaders of Iraqi Kurds this century) all have shaikhly antecedents, an asset even in the apparently secular business of nationalism, though it should be remembered that many shaikhs and their relatives have never used their position for temporal aggrandizement.

The shaikhs have achieved a quite extraordinary hold on the Kurdish community, with each village or tribal subsection tending to have its own loyalty to one or other order. So tenacious is this loyalty that although Mustafa Kemal Atatürk suppressed and proscribed all religious orders in modern Turkey as long ago as 1925, they continue to thrive underground, and have continued to be a significant obstacle to the efforts of socialists to mobilize the people along class lines.

Even since 1970, when leftist movements in Turkey started to make real inroads into Kurdish society, the unpoliticized have still voted for candidates who are chiefs or shaikhs, or possess these connections. Loyalty will persist despite an exploitative situation for a very long time. Even some Kurds who intellectually consider themselves 'progressive' can feel emotional loyalties to shaikh or chief. The support Shaikh Izzedin Husaini, admittedly himself sympathetic to the left, enjoys amongst extreme leftist Iranian Kurds today is just such an example.

The bonds of tribalism

Kurdish tribalism is far from homogeneous, and is now in a period of disintegration although tribal values are still strong. It is extremely difficult to classify Kurdish tribalism, since there is a complexity of relationship which changes almost from tribe to tribe. Beyond loyalty based on blood tie and territoriality lie the organization of tribal confederations, tribes and sub-tribes. It is almost impossible to generalize about these except to say that the difference is essentially one of degree rather than kind. Within the confederation, and even within the sub-tribe, there exist both blood-tie relationships and other ones based on mutual interest.

Loyalties of one group to another are not immutable, and can be severed and different ones negotiated, in response to political or economic situations. When an ambitious chief tries to extend his territory or the number of loyal groups within his control, there will almost certainly be a counter-move and shift of alliances as others endeavour to contain his ambition. This counter- move may be inspired by central government, or by neighbouring tribal groups who do not wish the 'equilibrium' disturbed. Thus when considering the underlying tension between the mountain and the plain (the desire and ability to maintain a greater degree of independence from government than plainspeople can), the potential and reality of alliance between a mountain tribe and government against another tribe must always be borne in mind.

It would seem that the tribal confederations, the largest tribal groupings, were originally created or fostered by the state, and formalized by the Ottomans and later the Persians, in order to guard the border marches. The Jaf confederation in southern Kurdistan is a prime example. The paramount chief accepted by the tribes also received official title from the state, thus drawing him closer to the state apparatus. He also nearly always claimed foreign descent, sometimes including *sayyid* (descent from the Prophet) status. In some cases the paramount family had no blood relationship whatsoever with members of the confederation. These two attributes, government recognition and noble, semi-religious origins, gave him a position above and outside the internal politics of the tribe, making his position as arbiter of internal disputes immensely strong.

One might wonder why the settlement of disputes is so important. But in Kurdish society, like others dependent on strong blood ties, a quarrel between two people is almost a contradiction in terms. No relative of someone in a dispute can easily stand apart since he is required to take his kinsman's part. Thus all disputes take on a dangerous factional quality. The need to settle such disputes within the tribe is always urgent before it is torn apart. That can only be done by the chief or some other respected and impartial (or theoretically so) individual. Many paramount chiefs surrounded themselves with a 'praetorian guard', who had no blood loyalty with others in the confederation, and who could provide the core of the confederation's fighting capacity.

Within the confederation were the tribes consisting of smaller groups, the land-owning or territory-controlling (in a nomadic sense) village groupings, descending mainly from a common real or fictitious patrilineal ancestor, but with other non-relative members of the village. The economy of these was based until 1920 almost exclusively on grazing flocks and illegal trading (and banditry) in the frontier region between the Ottoman and Persian Empires. For example, the Harki tribe would take Iranian salt to Iraq and bring back wheat to Iran, migrating annually from home near Urmiya to find winter fodder on the plain near Arbil.

Kurdish society on the plain and in the foothills differs so markedly from that of mountain Kurds that in many respects it can be treated as a separate culture. The plain economy was and is sedentary, combining some pastoralism with the more important business of growing of wheat, tobacco, barley and rice. Blood ties do frequently exist but they are not so all-embracing as amongst tribes with a nomadic tradition, and even those that might call themselves a tribe are usually subject to a wholly unrelated landlord family that has title to the land from the government and claims no bonds of loyalty with those who work its land. The relationship was and remains far more directly exploitative than that of the paramount chief in the mountains ever was, because the landlord was frequently an absentee, did not rely on his peasantry to fight for him, and could call on government forces to quell dissent. The landlord family has responsibilities primarily to government, and traditionally may have been in a vassal gift-exchange relationship with government, being recognized by the latter as fief-holder on condition it provided taxes and dues, and probably conscripts. The tribal people under it, whilst practising loyalty between themselves, might well be in a relationship akin to serfdom with the fief-holding family.

Some of these people formed sub-tribes, related to tribes up in the mountain. Others did not, and many were peasants without any tribal ties at all. All, however, were more similar to the other villages of the plains and foothills close to the mountains, both Christian and Arab Muslim villages, than they were to the mountain Kurds. These lowlanders viewed the mountain Kurds with the same apprehension as they did the desert Arabs. Some suffered from both, the beduin driven north by the heat for summer grazing, and Kurds driven down the mountain in winter. Sometimes peasants would burn off the grass before the mountain Kurds could bring their animals down to the lowlands for winter pasture.

Apart from the rural peasantry, there evolved the urbanized or 'civilized' Kurds, who were largely subsumed into the predominant culture of the plain. Unless they were absentee landlords (a growing phenomenon in the 20th Century), these have been natural opponents of the tribal chiefs, both as the first systematic purveyors of national ideas, and as people regarding tribalism as backward compared with urban government and administration. In addition to this urban educated class, a new 'oil proletariat' has also grown, both in Iraq and in Turkey. In this sense the Kurdish nationalist struggle during the 20th Century has been one not only between Kurd and non-Kurd rulers, but also between the concept of tribal rule and modern government, the land of insolence against the land of docility, a struggle which has split and weakened the Kurdish movement.

The power of the aghas

Although most tribes formed confederations, effective political power tended to lie more in the hands of *aghas*, as the chiefs were known, controlling either one village or a small group of them. The authority of confederate 'paramount chiefs' depended both on governmental recognition and on the willingness of these lower-ranking chiefs to do his bidding. These were reluctant to sacrifice their own power to his.

It is easy to appreciate the power of these village aghas. Most villages, certainly within the central Zagros area, depended upon authority and discipline for their viability. Someone had to ensure the equitable allocation and maintenance of the agricultural terraces, carefully maintained for millennia, and decide where and when the livestock should be taken to graze in winter, and above all how the water resources were to be shared.[12] That someone was, and still frequently is, the village agha. His authority must be beyond question if the village is to run smoothly.

Why has the village accepted his authority? An obvious reason is because discipline is self-evidently essential for a viable society. But another equally important reason is that as many as 50% of the village may be close relatives, and most of the remainder related in some way. If one wonders why the agha should enjoy such a large number of close relatives, forming the bedrock of social solidarity, the reason lies in the fact that the aghas until quite recently tended to be polygamous, whilst other villagers would almost always be monogamous. Families of aghas thus increased, whilst those of commoners remained static or even perhaps declined.

This simple fact explains why nearly everyone in the village is related to one another, and also why – despite despotism or exploitation – an agha's power and authority has remained so tenacious. His power of approval allows him to ensure that villagers do not marry outside the village, thus ensuring that the only relationships beyond the village boundary are controlled by himself, partly through his own judicious marriages to the daughters of neighbouring chiefs. He even controlled contact with visitors to the village, since it was only in the agha's guest house (a place well provisioned by all the villagers) that a stranger could be received.

Because he could thus effectively insulate the villagers from ties with the outside world, the agha alone handled diplomacy both with other villages and with the government. Here, if anywhere, the agha was vulnerable to the machinations of an ambitious relative. For hundreds of years a tradition of government recognition has been a valuable confirmation of village or tribal process. Withdrawal of that recognition, or support to a young pretender, could threaten an agha's position. In the 15th Century the Turkoman dynasties, the Karakoyunlu, Aqkoyunlu and Safavids, successfully appointed Kurdish chiefs, killing those appointed by the previous dynasty. Relations with government and with neighbouring chiefs were interrelated. Thus as recently as the 1974-75 Iraqi-Kurdish war, whilst an estimated 50,000 Kurds fought against the government, tens of thousands of irregulars fought for it. In a situation where tenure of the chiefship is not guaranteed, many aghas would have been at risk if the rebel chiefs had defeated the army and persuaded the government to recognize a new order in the mountains.

The importance of land

As in most societies, control of land is a critical component of power. In the mountains, land was traditionally controlled by the tribe, and the agha held in trust the responsibility for the equitable allocation of pastoral rights. On the plain and in the foothills, the community worked on land held in fief, or later directly owned, by a landlord who shared neither common lineage nor common economic interest with those who worked it.

During the mid-19th Century, however, the reform in land holding started a process of 'detribalizing' land, reinforcing the position of both landlord and mountain agha as titleholders over much previously commonly held land. This process happened on both the Ottoman and Persian sides of the border, increasing stratification within the tribe, reducing communal features of the tribal economy, and encouraging a new class of absentee landlords who frequently co-operated with tribal chiefs still in the mountain to ensure their common interests. The transition at the beginning of the 20th Century from a subsistence to a market economy intensified these interests and accelerated absorption of the landlord class into the state establishment.

After 1920 in Iraq and Iran, the spread of land registration put title to land in the name of individuals so that it became effectively their absolute property. This gave new strength to the agha class, whilst tribespeople became increasingly a landless cultivator class. This process was made a good deal easier since the creation of more impermeable international borders after 1920 destroyed the nomadic pattern of many tribes which had seasonally crossed the mountains. In Iran this was accompanied by forcible settlement of the nomads by the Shah. By the 1960s, 78% of cultivated land in Iranian Kurdistan was registered as privately owned, only 2% remaining 'tribal'. In Turkey, the transition from tribal to capitalist economy produced a situation by 1965 where 62% of the 800,000 farmers of the Kurdish area were landholders, but of these only 2% owned 30.5% of cultivable land, whilst the remaining 60% of landholders owned only 19%.

It was inevitable that this process should, in all three countries, draw the new landlord class into the ruling establishment. Direct government increased the power of village aghas, since their relationship with government was no longer regulated through confederate paramount chiefs. Tribespeople allowed their aghas to register tribal land in the agha's name, partly because both agha and tribesman were ignorant of the implications, and also because of the widespread aversion of being registered, since this always meant an increased governmental hold on individual families for taxation and – worse yet – conscription into the army.

The comparatively recent advent of mechanization of agriculture on fertile plains has resulted in only seasonal work for the villager. This has led to seasonal migration to nearby or even distant towns (as far as Ankara or Baghdad) for employment. This migration has been intensified by land scarcity and underdevelopment of Kurdish areas, creating the more solid phenomenon of permanent absence from the village for working males. The growth of a Kurdish proletariat, and industrial capital, outside Kurdistan has had an inevitable effect on the simplistic picture of Kurdish life described above. In the last 20 years or so the position of the agha has been eroded by these socio-economic factors far more than by any efforts of the state. But it is extremely important to remember the power of tradition, and that the advance of these socio-economic changes has occurred unevenly and is still under way.

Before turning to the bloody and colourful history of the Kurdish people, one further point must be made:

> *The tales of all the raids and feuds and wars in these mountains,...*
> *deeds of daring, self-sacrifice, greed and treachery form the subject for*
> *Kurdish epic songs, which the young warrior hears as he lies awake in*
> *his cradle. One cannot fail to be impressed by the thorough indoctrina-*
> *tion in the heroics of bloodletting that young Kurds, among other*
> *mountaineers, undergo.*[13]

Those deeds, not least the modern nationalist movement, pass into a potent folklore which is still a major part of the political education of young Kurds today.

3

HIDDEN FROM HISTORY
– THE KURDS BEFORE 1920

urdistan's people, like those in other unruly areas, have lived in tension with central government authority – and frequently with each other. Like the beduin, they have attracted the romantic affection of European travellers and often been explicitly described as 'superior' to the 'peasantry' around them. It is a dangerous assumption. Nevertheless, there is no doubting the distinctiveness of the culture:

> '... just as proud, independent and thievish as their ancestors. They are as devotedly attached to their mountains as the Scotch or Swiss, and like the former, they are divided into clans or sects, acknowledging the supremacy of their chiefs, who are regarded with the same devotion, and followed with the same blind zeal which used to distinguish the Highlanders in former days. They are proud, haughty, and overbearing exactly in proportion to their ignorance, and like our own clans of old, despise more or less all arts but those of war and plunder, and all professions but that of arms.'[14]

However bigoted he may seem, this 19th Century traveller was undoubtedly accurate in his assessment. Banditry on the highways and byways against all travellers (Kurds and others) was viewed until quite recently as a legitimate and indispensable source of income for some tribes. Nor can one doubt for a moment that the Kurds were a constant threat to the plains. Xenophon was not the only one to run into trouble. There are numerous references throughout the Arab period and thereafter to Kurdish revolt and depredations. Nevertheless, these outbreaks of fighting frequently indicated that a carefully evolved relationship had gone awry.

Kurdish semi-autonomy

Like central government, the Kurds generally wanted a quiet life, in which they could trade what they had to offer – skins, livestock, oak galls and other materials – in return for their needs. Their frequent use of middlemen to ply this trade increased their dependence on the centres of states incorporating Kurdistan. Successive governors in the surrounding area throughout the medieval period offered recognition of their semi-autonomous status to the Kurdish aghas. A few of these, most notably the Marwanids of Diyarbekir, Akhlat and Malazgird, achieved total autonomy (983-1096 AD), but the majority remained in a 'gift-exchange' relationship, one that became increasingly formalized from the Saljuq period (11th Century) onwards.

The gifts the Kurdish aghas had to offer were tribute (frequently only nominal) and troops. The aghas themselves frequently led these contingents and, if not, they appointed those who did. By this process aghas tied themselves into the regional governing establishment, and co-operated in the creation of a governing class of feudal lords which overlaid blood loyalties within the tribe with 'feudal' ones, formalizing concepts of rank within Kurdish society and forging formal ties with the outside world. By the 14th Century there was a distinct military aristocracy controlling the nomad tribes, a settled provincial nobility, a civil service (however rudimentary that might have been), and a religious class who shared like the others an interest in their opposite numbers on the plain. Those who provided and led Kurdish troops frequently settled outside Kurdistan, whilst others, like Kurdistan's most celebrated son, Saladin, were not born in Kurdistan, and never lived there. He was a product of the Kurd military aristocracy.

Most of the tribes at this stage were either wholly or partly nomadic, moving to uplands in summer, but coming onto lower ground during the cold months. These nomadic tribes benefited from the social and economic upheavals resulting from the destruction of the peasantry by the Mongols and Turkomans in the 13th and 14th Century. They inherited as grazing land large tracts of previously agricultural land in Anatolia, and were able to penetrate into Armenian regions for the first time.

The struggle between the Ottoman and Safavid Empires, newly emerged in Turkey and Persia respectively during the 16th Century, allowed the Kurdish tribes and their chiefs to formalize their position and importance further. Following the decisive victory of the Ottoman Sultan Selim over the Safavid Shah Isma'il at Chaldiran in central Anatolia in 1514, the Kurdish aghas assisted in throwing Isma'il out of eastern Anatolia, and establishing what, after the treaty of 1639, became a durable border between the Ottoman and Persian worlds. Most of the Kurdish tribes sided with the Ottomans since the latter offered the chiefs fiefdoms, and to some principalities (*emirates*) in return for undertaking a formalized role of policing virtually the whole border. These fiefdoms and principalities were largely sited in the border marches themselves.

Fifteen main emirates were created, and provided the overall political structure of Kurdistan until the 19th Century. Each of these was ruled by a family granted hereditary title by government which claimed, through its local governor, which family member actually held office as *emir*. Whilst this might seem an admirable arrangement for allowing Kurdish society considerable freedom to continue undisturbed, it gave the state an extremely important hold on key positions, for in most families there was usually a brother or cousin ready to do the state's bidding if the incumbent agha proved rebellious. The tension between family and individual interest is still a potent one. During the 1974 war in Iraqi Kurdistan, a significant number of 'pretenders' within their tribe either stayed at home or actively helped the government rather than join the Kurdish rebels. Old habits die hard.

Despite their closer cultural ties to Iran, the Kurds were discouraged from supporting the Persian Safavids because of the latter's severe treatment of aghas who had acted for preceding dynasties, their increasing Shi'ite distinctiveness inherited from the preceding Aq Koyunlu dynasty, and their attempts at direct government.

Extension of direct Ottoman control

The arrangement collapsed in the first half of the 19th Century when regular Ottoman administration was extended into Kurdistan. It was part of the attempt by Istanbul, following the destruction of the janissaries, to reinvigorate the machinery of Empire, and to ensure sufficiently firm control so that the successful attempts at independence in the Balkans would not be repeated elsewhere. The interest and involvement of the Europeans in Balkan liberation was a cause for alarm, particularly since a number of European traders, missionaries and consuls were beginning to penetrate different parts of the Empire. In the Caucasus and eastern Anatolia, Russian intentions and border incursions were a cause for Ottoman concern and necessitated the raising of conscripts.

The extension of direct Ottoman control, with its implicit destruction of the old emirates, was resisted by a succession of revolts by the

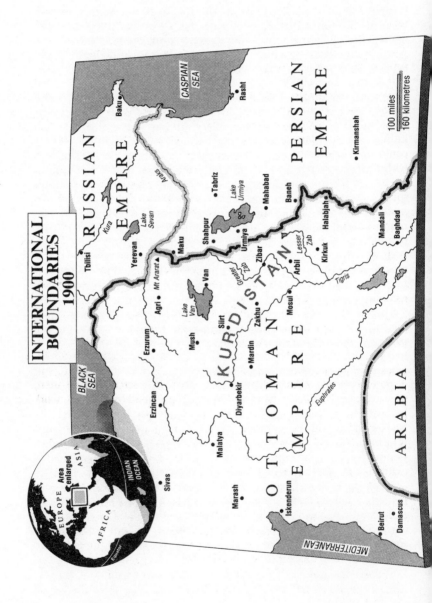

emirs. Some attempted to assert complete independence, others tried to hold onto what they could. One or two tried to play off the two regional superpowers without success, lessons for the future in the dangers of rebellion on the frontier between the two regional powers. A rebellious chief might alienate one, but it was essential to enjoy the support, or benevolent neutrality, of the other.

It is easy to see the risings of the Kurdish emirs as the first great movement of Kurdish nationalism, expressed in traditional ways, and harking back to an illusory 'golden age' of Kurdish freedom. But it would be foolish to assume more than that these risings by powerful individuals were largely to do with their own power, and that they could be as reluctant to co-operate with each other as they became with the regional powers that held them in.

The destruction of the emirates had profound effects on Kurdish society and politics, breaking down 'power bases' into very much smaller segments. Secular power was inherited by the considerable number of aghas, the old tribal chiefs, most of whom controlled only a handful of villages. In the absence of strong authority such as had been exerted by the emirs, the Ottoman administrators were a poor substitute when it came to dealing with 'internal' matters. There was frequently disorder and rivalry between the aghas in the absence of a recognized structure of arbitration.

This vacuum was filled by religious leaders. In the past, whilst enjoying the respect of the secular authorities, the men of religion had not participated to any great degree in political life. In the disorder that had grown by the mid 19th Century within Kurdish society, the religious shaikhs were being called upon increasingly to act as arbiters in disputes between aghas, villages, and tribes. Respected as holy men, they were well suited to be mediators. These shaikhs did not work independently, but usually belonged to one of two dervish orders, the Naqshbandis and the Qadiris. Both orders, but particularly the Naqshbandis, had grown rapidly in the first three decades of the 19th Century.[15] These networks cut across tribal lines and therefore were extremely powerful coherent forces in a peculiarly fragmented society.

It was perhaps no accident that the next major revolt, in 1880, was led by a religious leader, Shaikh Ubaydallah of the Naqshbandi order, and enjoyed broader support than hitherto. Ubaydallah called for an autonomous Kurdish entity, marking perhaps the real beginning of some still vague idea of the Kurds being one single nation. In 1878 he had written to the local British Vice-Consul:

'The Kurdish nation is a people apart. Their religion is different and their laws and customs are distinct... The chiefs and rulers of Kurdistan, whether Turkish or Persian subjects, and the inhabitants of Kurdistan one and all are agreed that matters cannot be carried on in this way with the two governments.'[16]

But such agreement did not exist either within the Kurdish community or beyond it. Although he enjoyed wide support amongst Kurds on both sides of the Perso-Ottoman border, this was more to do with quasi-millennarian expectations amongst his followers. When Shaikh Ubaydallah attempted to prove his words in the reality of rebellion, Sultan and Shah co-operated in his defeat, helped by Kurdish tribes hostile to his ambitions.

Despite what Ubaydallah might have to say, many Kurdish aghas were still ready to assist Istanbul in upholding the Sultan's authority and the established order. They provided tribesmen to fill the ranks of the new Hamidiya cavalry raised in 1891 as a militia force to police eastern Anatolia and the Russian border. In part this was because the chiefs commanded their own tribesmen in the Hamidiya, and were able to assert themselves in their area, salaried by the Sultan. They were unlikely to be punished for depredations against villagers, whether these were Christian or Muslim, Armenian or Kurd.

It was also because they shared a common Sunni Muslim identity with the Ottoman establishment, and they shared the latter's fear of the growing separatist expressions of the Armenian community amongst whom many Kurds lived. With Russia quite clearly thinking in terms of encouraging Armenian separatism and of advancing its borders to reach or absorb Armenian areas, the Kurdish aghas willingly assisted Ottoman repression of Armenian communities, which reached a nightmare climax in 1895-96. Kurdish families moved into many of the villages from which Armenians had been eliminated.

The Young Turks and the Kurds

The Young Turk revolution of 1908, which overthrew the despotic rule of Sultan Abdulhamid, promising constitutional reform and representative participation in government to all the peoples of the Ottoman Empire, did not fulfil expectations. In the first euphoria, a number of political clubs were established by Kurdish intellectuals, aghas (who had received some education) and officers in Istanbul, Mosul, Diyarbekir, Bitlis, Mush, Erzerum and even Baghdad, and a few schools that taught in Kurdish were founded. Some of the political clubs established contact with the tribes in their *vilayet* (province). The first Kurdish newspaper was published in Cairo, then in London and – of all places – Folkestone, from 1898.

But these currents neither grew into a coherent political movement nor unified the Kurdish people. Instead a new conflict appeared within Kurdish society, between urban intellectuals and the aghas. The latter were naturally uneasy about the implications of political clubs and schools that taught Kurdish, since political education and literacy could both eventually threaten their position within Kurdish society. The first Kurdish 'Society for Progress and Mutual Aid' was formed in 1908 by representatives of two outstanding Kurdish families. Rivalries between these founding families in Istanbul, the Badr Khans and the Sayyid Abd al Qadirs, for leadership of the movement gave way to informing on each other's 'liberal' activities, and the Ottoman authorities had no difficulty in closing the society down. It is unlikely that many traditionally minded aghas were upset when other such ventures were closed down with the outbreak of World War I in 1914.

When the Ottomans went to war, it was against the European powers, particularly Russia. It was therefore natural that the majority of Kurds, as Ottoman citizens, as Sunni Muslims, and as neighbours of the Armenians whose loyalty remained in doubt, should accept conscription and serve. In 1915 some Kurds helped to kill and expel Armenians from Kurdish areas and when they had the chance the more nationally-minded amongst the latter took equally bloody revenge. Nevertheless, the government extended the persecution of minorities to include Kurdish villages in Bitlis and Erzerum provinces during the winter of 1916-17. It feared the Kurds might make common cause with the Russian enemy on the north-eastern front.[17] So deportations of Kurds were begun, with many dying of exposure as they marched westwards away from the sensitive region in the depth of winter. They slept out in the rain and snow, those surviving the night burying those who did not.

The peace settlement of 1918 and after

It was a radically different world which awaited the Kurds in 1918, one that had little resemblance to the one which had gone to war four years earlier. The Ottoman Empire was defeated, prostrate and with foreign armies encamped on much of its territories, with British forces occupying almost all of present-day Iraq, including some of the Kurdish areas. Beyond the Empire's borders much else had happened: Austria-Hungary had collapsed; western Persia endured the presence of

Turkish, Russian and British forces confronting each other in the strategic zone around Azerbaijan and the Caucasus; Tsarist Russia had been overthrown by the Bolsheviks. Allied plans for post-war settlement included the apportionment of Turkish parts of the Empire to Greece, Russia, Italy and France. These remained almost entirely a dead letter because of the collapse of Tsarist Russia during the war and because Turkey's defeat triggered a major internal upheaval inside Turkey.

An entirely different struggle was also to take place. This was between the expressed or unexpressed strategic or imperial interests of the powers with military force still at their command in the area, and the principles of civilization accepted in a general sense at the conference table by these same powers – so long as they did not interfere with their own plans. These principles were set out most clearly by President Woodrow Wilson in his Fourteen Point Programme for World Peace, Point Twelve of which stated that non-Turkish minorities of the Ottoman Empire should be:

> *'assured of an absolute unmolested opportunity of autonomous development'.*

It was an admirable if unrealistic aspiration to create a just order in the Middle East. The Kurdish people were ill-prepared to face the challenge of the post-war settlement and the new nationalism. Most of them still believed in membership of the Sunni community, the basis of Ottoman society irrespective of language or race, and an identity only broken later by the struggle within the remnants of the Ottoman Empire between the last defenders of the *ancien régime* and the challenging reformists led by Mustafa Kemal Atatürk. Internally the Kurds were weakened by the traditional structures under which most of them continued to live. Tribal loyalty remained far stronger for village or pastoralist Kurds than new ideas about a Kurdish nation. Aghas were a good deal more concerned with holding or increasing their position locally than with uniting with old adversaries in neighbouring valleys, or with those urban Kurds more capable of negotiating with the outside world.

The intellectuals tried, as they had done before the war, to establish political groups that would further Kurdish independence or at least autonomy. Of these the most important was *Kurdistan Taali Djemiyeti* (Society for the Recovery of Kurdistan), which enjoyed the leadership of Kurdistan's most illustrious emigres in Istanbul. It was not long, however, before the society was split between autonomists, who believed that Kurds should stand by the Turks, and those who strove for complete independence. Aware that the Allies were considering the establishment of an independent Armenian state (the Great Powers had a deservedly uneasy conscience about their feeble efforts to protect the Armenians previously), and that if such a state were established it would be at Kurdish expense, a group of Kurds led by General Sharif Pasha co-operated with Armenians in the presentation of a joint memorandum to the Peace Conference in Paris in 1919.

The outcome of these deliberations, the Treaty of Sèvres, signed on 20 August 1920, brought the Kurds and the Armenians closer to statehood than ever before or since. The relevant parts of the treaty stated that a commission composed of Allied appointees would:

> *'prepare for local autonomy in those regions where the Kurdish element is preponderant lying east of the Euphrates, to the south of the still-to-be established Armenian frontier and to the north of the frontier between Turkey, Syria and Mesopotamia' (Article 62);*

> *'If, after one year has elapsed since the implementation of the present treaty, the Kurdish population of the areas designated in Article 62 calls on the Council of the League of Nations and demonstrates that a majority of the population in these areas wishes to become independent of Turkey, and if the Council then estimates that the population in question is capable of such independence and recommends that it be granted, then Turkey agrees, as of now, to comply with this recommendation and to renounce all rights and titles to the area... If and when the said renunciation is made, no objection shall be raised by the main Allied powers should the Kurds living in that part of Kurdistan at present included in the vilayet of Mosul seek to become citizens of the newly independent Kurdish state' (Article 64).*

This last sentence was a clear reference to Britain's occupation of the vilayet of Mosul on account of its oil resources, carried out four days after it had agreed an armistice with the Ottoman Government in 1918, but not accepted by the Turks until 1925.

Although the Allies had hedged their promise about with a number of conditions which made independence conditional on the goodwill of governments who had themselves strategic interests in the area, the Kurds had some reason to be optimistic about the promises offered them. If anything there were grounds for doubting their own ability to demonstrate their 'capability of independence', given the serious internal weaknesses of Kurdish society.

Had the Council of the newly created League of Nations granted independence, would the Kurds have forged a nation out of their tribes? Would they and the Armenians have succeeded in agreeing a mutual border without external supervision and enforcement, or would they have been plunged into conflict?[18] These questions must remain unanswered, because events in Turkey itself rendered the Treaty of Sèvres a dead letter before it could be implemented

4

THE KURDS IN TURKEY
– THE LEGACY OF ATATÜRK

The defeated Ottoman government in Istanbul which had signed the Treaty of Sèvres did not survive to implement it. The seizure of its Arab territories of Syria and Mesopotamia, the threat of the loss of eastern Anatolia to a new Armenian and possibly a Kurdish state, the entry into Cilician Anatolia of a French force intent on annexing it to Syria, and most of all the abject failure of the government in Istanbul to respond to the invasion of Ottoman Turkey by the Greeks, of whom large numbers were to be found in Thrace (European Turkey) and in western Anatolia, had already resulted in a revolt in Anatolia led by Mustafa Kemal, who had distinguished himself against the Allies at Gallipoli.

The regime of Kemal Atatürk

The support of a significant proportion of Kurds for Mustafa Kemal's revolt indicated their identity with the other Muslims of Anatolia and their fears of falling within an Armenian, and therefore Christian, state. Kemal himself had been careful to appeal, despite his own Turkish nationalist views, to Muslim unity and to a Muslim Fatherland. Kurdish forces under Turkish officers defeated and drove out the troops of *Menshevik* Georgia and *Dashnak* Armenia.

In the west Mustafa Kemal Atatürk established undisputed leadership of the nation by his defeat of the Greeks and the elimination of virtually all Christians remaining in Anatolia. The Allies found themselves having to renegotiate the settlement of the remnants of an empire which had ceased to exist. Although they themselves kept virtually all that they had wanted (France conceded Cilician Anatolia to Atatürk), they were not prepared to negotiate for the Armenians, or for the Kurds. They knew that to implement these aspects of Sèvres would require military enforcement in a difficult climate and country. It was more than the Allies, exhausted in World War I and satisfied with their own gains, were prepared to do. They also now wanted Turkey as a bulwark against Bolshevism.

They therefore arranged a new peace conference at Lausanne in November 1922, finalized in treaty in July 1923, whereby Turkey, alone of those defeated in the conflict, managed to impose terms on the victors. It re-established complete and undivided sovereignty over eastern Thrace and all Anatolia, though the question of the disputed Mosul vilayet was left unsettled for the time being.

The Kurds had fought for the Ottoman Empire, not for a specifically Turkish state. Despite official statements of recognition of 'the national and social rights of the Kurds',[19] it quickly became clear that Atatürk's interest following the defeat of the Christian elements was in the creation of a nation-state along European and authoritarian lines, and it was a specifically Turkish and secular state that he intended. The Kurds of Turkey very quickly lost their special identity and the status they had enjoyed as fellow Muslims.

In contrast to the Treaty of Sèvres, no reference was made in the Lausanne treaty to the Kurds by name. The abolition of the Sultanate in 1922, and of the Caliphate in 1924, removed the twin pillars on which the idea could be sustained that they, as fellow citizens and Muslims, albeit Kurdish ones, alongside Turkish Muslims had liberated Islamic Anatolia from the Armenian and Greek threat. These abolitions also removed the temporal and spiritual bases from which the authority of aghas and shaikhs, however indirectly, derived. On the day of the abolition of the Caliphate, 3 March 1924, all public vestiges of separate Kurdish identity were crushed. Kurdish schools, associations, publications, religious fraternities and teaching foundations were all banned.

Thus two factors, the threat to Kurdish identity, and the threat to the traditional order of aghas and shaikhs (through the destruction of Sultanate and Caliphate) served to unify many Kurds of different viewpoints. Within a short space of time an informal movement embraced not only politically aware urban intellectuals, but also many aghas and the shaikhs (who were able to mobilize large numbers of men through the religious orders). However, this unity was fragile.

In 1925 widespread revolt erupted under the leadership of a Naqshbandi, Shaikh Said of Piran, following the massacre of a Turkish detachment sent to Piran to arrest his followers. Shaikh Said himself was of considerable importance, being local head of the order, custodian of an important pilgrimage site, and in matrimonial alliance with a number of Kurdish chiefs. He was a classic example of those shaikhs able to wield both secular and religious power. His rallying cry was nationalist, but almost certainly those who responded did so because of long-standing religious and secular loyalties. It is noteworthy that his supporters were overwhelmingly Zaza-speaking Kurds, and that few others rallied to his cause.

The rising quickly revealed weakness within Kurdish ranks. Although the rebels overran about one third of Kurdish Anatolia, they were unable to capture any towns of size. Urban Kurdish notables failed to respond in Diyarbekir, where there had been quite a lively nationalist association. When the rebels besieged this important town, those inside who harboured Kurd nationalist feeling did so behind closed doors only, except for a handful of lower-class fellow Zazas related to the rebels outside the walls. The rebels failed to invite the substantial number of non-tribal Kurds, oppressed tenants and share-croppers around Diyarbekir, to join the revolt, because they were contemptuously deemed unfit to fight.

Turkish troops were rushed to the east, their movement facilitated by their being allowed to travel by train through French-held territory, and by mid-April they had crushed the rising. Ruthless suppression of the area and of the dervish orders throughout Turkey followed. Shaikh Said and hundreds of his supporters were hanged, hundreds of villages were burnt to the ground, and thousands of peasants, anything between 40,000 and 250,000, died in the 'pacification'. In addition Ankara decided to denude the area of its Kurdish population and commenced the forced movement of thousands from their homes.

Almost immediately another revolt broke out, this time further north around the foothills of Mount Ararat, led by local aghas and supported from outside by a new Kurdish liberation organization, *Khoyboun*, based in Lebanon and Syria, which succeeded in bringing together all the leading Kurdish groups to co-ordinate support for the rising. It was the first time a nationalist organization, rather than a shaikh or agha, had taken so central a role. Of equal significance, the insurgents enjoyed the support of the Shah of Iran, Reza Shah. By the end of 1929 a sizeable area stretching between Bitlis, Van and Ararat was in the hands of a Kurdish administration which was strong enough for the Turkish government to consider negotiations. However, this was rendered unnecessary when it reached an agreement with the Shah, who cut off assistance to the Kurds and allowed the Turkish forces to move through Iranian territory to encircle the Kurdish forces.

Nothing illustrates more clearly the free hand given to anyone prepared to assist in the suppression of the Kurds than Law No. 1850 published at this time:

'*Murders and other actions committed individually or collectively, from the 20th of June 1930 to the 10th of December 1930, by the representatives of the state or the province, by the military or civil authorities, by the local authorities, by guards or militiamen, or by any civilian having helped the above or acted on their behalf, during the pursuit and extermination of the revolts which broke out in Ercis, Zilan, Agridag [Ararat] and the surrounding areas, including Pulumur in Erzincan province and the area of the First Inspectorate [which covered all the provinces of Anatolian Kurdistan], will not be considered as crimes.*' (Article 1).[20]

The then Minister of Justice made clear the relationship of Turk and non-Turk in the state:

'*I believe that the Turk must be the only lord, the only master of this country. Those who are not of pure Turkish stock can have only one right in this country, the right to be servants and slaves.*'[21]

Yet again the Ankara government used mass deportation to pacify the area and assimilate the Kurds into the Turkish population, and legalized this mass deportation and the encouragement of Turks to settle in Anatolian Kurdistan on 5 May 1932. This law of 1932 legalized the total evacuation of certain areas. It was not surprising therefore that in one area which was designated for total evacuation but which had not yet been regained by the Turkish army, Kurdish resistance was renewed under local religious leadership. This area was Dersim (now called Tunceli), a relatively small area but one which kept three Turkish army corps engaged in guerrilla war until the end of 1938. Once again, repression was achieved only with the utmost brutality. Furthermore Kurdish villages were closely policed, and use of the Kurdish language, dress, folklore and names prohibited. The area remained under martial law until 1946.

The Kurds in post-Atatürk Turkey

Such measures and the threat of further atrocities against an unarmed civilian population silenced Kurdish nationalist activities for almost 30 years. Much of Anatolian Kurdistan became a 'military zone', ostensibly because of the proximity of the Soviet border, but in reality to deny it to its indigenous Kurds because of their recalcitrance. Perhaps over one million Kurds were forcibly displaced between 1925 and 1938, including aghas and shaikhs, the focus of local Kurdish solidarity, and young men who were conscripted into the army where they could be assimilated under duress. Indeed, it seemed as if the Kurds would accept assimilation as inevitable.

Life for the Kurdish community eased somewhat in 1950 with the first free general election, in which the Democratic Party was swept to power in reaction to almost 25 years of Kemalist authoritarianism. Kurds, in their deep antipathy to Kemalism, voted heavily for the Democratic Party, and were rewarded by the return of exiled aghas and shaikhs and the reinstatement of their property. These aghas, shaikhs and landlords acquired new importance since they could deliver votes to government and favours to the Kurdish population. Kurds were elected to Parliament; some even became ministers. Schools, roads and hospitals began to appear in the region.

The newly emergent Kurdish bourgeoisie, many of whom were the scions of the traditional leadership, espoused a new philosophy called *doguculuk* ('Eastism') which advocated economic development in the neglected east. In part it was a response to Kurdish activism elsewhere, especially in Iraq, and the exposure of eastern Anatolia to Kurdish-language radio broadcasts from neighbouring countries. But the proponents of Eastism were careful to work in Turkish and to avoid any reference to Kurds or Kurdistan, though no one could be in doubt what was in their mind. Fifty Kurdish leaders of this movement were arrested. There were limits to the Democratic Party's liberalization.

Following an army coup d'état in 1960 in response to Prime Minister Menderes's efforts to stifle parliamentary opposition, the situation for the Kurdish community improved further with the introduction of a new constitution in 1961, though not before thousands more dissidents had been deported by the military. This constitution allowed freedom of expression, of the press and of association. Kurds were able to express their dissent through Turkish structures, organizations, publications and so forth, writing in Turkish and even in Kurdish concerning the history, folklore and economic problems of the 'East', even though the authors risked imprisonment for their views.

There were aspects of Turkey's development as a modern nation-state which the regime could not deal with so easily. The banishment of so many Kurds, particularly those who by birth, education or political ambition posed a threat, had created a large urban population scattered across the cities of the Turkish state. They were far harder to deal with. As the cities of Turkey grew, so also did the new proletariat amongst whom the Kurds became very numerous, since there was little work for them in the neglected east. It was impossible for these thousands, indeed millions, to be insulated completely from awareness of

Kurds elsewhere asserting their identity, or of liberation movements further afield.

A clandestine party, the Kurdistan Democratic Party (KDPT), was established in 1965, echoing and in solidarity with Barzani's nationalist movement in Iraqi Kurdistan. Its supporters tended to be traditional in outlook, as Barzani's were in Iraq. Unlike the leftists who were more concerned with equal rights within the state, the KDPT was explicitly separatist. A number of leftist Turks showed an interest in the problem which successive regimes had tried to hide, and the Turkish Workers' Party welcomed Kurdish intellectuals, took up the Kurdish cause and established branches in Kurdistan itself.

Kurds, as Turks, were able to participate in political life so long as they claimed a Turkish identity. A number of deputies from the 'East' have been Kurdish. But they had to proceed with care, and had to belong to Turkish parties, since it was – and remains – illegal to form a specifically Kurdish party. When the Deputy for Diyarbekir, himself a Kurd and founder of the New Turkey Party, during his brief term as Minister of Health in the 1960s succeeded in building more hospitals and dispensaries in Kurdish areas than all the previous administrations put together, he was quickly forced to resign amidst accusations of regionalism and Kurdish nationalism. In April 1979 a Kurdish ex-minister of Public Works (under Prime Minister Ecevit) and long- standing member for Mardin created a scandal by publicly stating: 'In Turkey there are Kurds. I too am a Kurd.'[22] He was subsequently charged and tried by military court for 'propaganda aimed at weakening national feelings' and condemned to over two years' imprisonment with hard labour.

As Kurdish and Leftist groups became increasingly vocal and managed to draw in a far wider constituency, so the government increased its efforts to silence cultural and political activity of which it did not approve. Many of the bilingual Kurdish-Turkish journals that had appeared in the mid-1960s were prohibited by decree of the Demirel government in January 1967, and their editors arrested. As Demirel's repression increased from 1967 onwards, with the use of special commando groups to patrol Kurdistan and intimidate the population and ransack the homes of suspects, Kurdish students and militants (apparently close to the Turkish Workers' Party) called for mass demonstrations, which took place on 3 August 1967. More than 10,000 turned out in Silvan, and over 25,000 in Diyarbekir – the first expression of Kurdish anger for 30 years. Such demonstrations only made the government more implacable and more brutal in the enforcement of its authority, particularly around Batman and Silvan, where important oil deposits exist.

There was good reason for governmental unease. In 1969, first in Ankara, then in Istanbul and in the Kurdish towns of the east, an Organization of Revolutionary Kurdish Youth (DDKO) had set up Eastern Revolutionary Cultural Centres. Many of its leaders were members of the Turkish Workers' Party. The proliferation of leftist groups in Turkey and the support they enjoyed in Kurdistan led to violent confrontation with rightist groups who were frequently backed by local police. Political murders became commonplace between bitter adversaries of left and right. Meanwhile the Turkish Workers' Party had officially changed its stand on the Kurdish question, in October 1970 becoming the first legal party to recognize the Kurds' struggle. Recognition of the Kurds (though it did not go so far as advocating self-government) led to the party being banned.

5

THE KURDS IN TURKEY
– REPRESSION IN THE 1970s AND 1980s

The army overthrew the Demirel government in March 1971. Thousands of arrests took place all over Turkey, but particularly in the east on account, it was claimed, of a planned Kurdish uprising. Murder and torture were widely reported. Many were accused of belonging to the Democratic Party of Kurdistan or to DDKO, which was banned forthwith. Oppression of the Kurdish population continued erratically throughout the 1970s. The conflict between rightists and leftists had not ceased but pervaded to some extent the instruments of government authority, the army, the police and the judiciary.

This weakness ended with the 1979 proclamation of martial law in the Kurdish provinces and the resumption of consistently repressive measures. The immediate reasons for the proclamation were the rumours of armed Kurdish freedom fighters (*pesh mergas*) seizing areas and declaring them 'liberated' zones, but it was also on account of the development of a more or less overt Kurdish nationalism, in which Diyarbekir had become the main centre of activity. As the Turkish President said:

> 'there is no room for liberated regions and activities aimed at language, racial, class or sectarian differences in our homeland. The government will defeat the disease and heads will be crushed.'[23]

In the following years urban-based political groups were repressed a good deal more easily than rural ones. In September 1979 the Turkish newspaper *Hurriyet* reported that 5000 Turkish Kurds had been recruited to fight alongside Iranian Kurds. Although publicly denied by the government, this report followed the interception by the army of a convoy of arms apparently destined for fellow Kurds in Iran. Unlike the Iranian and Iraqi governments, which recognize that the Kurds are a distinct community (even if that does not guarantee any special rights), the Turkish government could not possibly allow support or any contact whatever to occur between its own Kurds and those elsewhere, since it would encourage Kurdish consciousness inside Turkey. Even in a situation of conflict between Turkey and one of its neighbours, the Turkish government would act with utmost caution before playing their Kurdish 'card'. In this respect they differ radically from their neighbours Iraq and Iran in their attitude to the Kurds.

In September 1980, as in 1960 and in 1971, a group of army generals carried out another coup d'état. They made it clear that they intended to brook no expression of the Kurdish movement or identity whatsoever. Indeed, the very first speeches made by General Evren, leader of the Junta, and Prime Minister Ulusu were in Kurdistan. A spate of specious articles appeared in academic and other journals arguing that the Kurds were true Turks – *Turkkurtleri* – merely another of the Central Asiatic Turkic tribes from which the Turkish people are derived.

The ban on Kurdish was implemented more strictly than ever, villages and homes were raided by the army, and tens of thousands of people, primarily Leftist activists and Kurds, were arrested and interrogated, frequently under torture. Indeed, by the end of the decade it was generally thought that approximately half of the 250,000 or so civilians arrested by the authorities on security grounds were in fact Kurdish.

The PKK and the state response: 1979-1988

Meanwhile the conflict with armed Kurdish nationalists entered an entirely new phase. This was signalled by the emergence of the radical Kurdistan Workers' Party (PKK). The PKK had been in operation since the late 1970s, formed by disaffected Kurdish students, led by Abdallah Ocalan. It was composed of the most marginalized elements of Kurdish society, people who felt 'excluded from the country's social and economic development'.[24] They believed that other Kurdish parties had compromised, and that nothing short of outright victory and the independence of a socialist Kurdish state would solve their problems.

The Turkish state correctly recognized the PKK as the single most serious threat to state security, and was stringent with those PKK members it captured. By 1985 it had demanded the death sentence in over 600 cases in mass trials. It also took strong measures in the field, militarizing the whole of eastern and south-eastern Anatolia. Two of Turkey's four armies were based in the region, and by 1990 it was still reckoned that over 150,000 troops were in the region.

Ostensibly Turkey argued, as it had done since the 1960s, that this military concentration, including NATO and US military installations, was on account of the continued sensitivity of the borders with the USSR and Iran, and the general latent instability of the 'northern tier' stretching across to Afghanistan. In reality, Kurdish irredentism was perceived as a greater threat. Indeed, apart from its short experiences in the Korean war and in Cyprus (1974), the Turkish army's only battle experience since the establishment of the Republic had been against Kurdish guerrillas.

The restoration of civil authority under Prime Minister Turgut Özal in 1984 had no immediate effect on the conflict between the government and its Kurdish population. In August 1984 a new and more dangerous phase opened with a PKK attack on the town centres of Eruh and Shemdinli, in which 24 soldiers and nine civilians were killed. The following month another 12 soldiers were killed. The security forces responded by the arrest of over 1000 suspects. These guerrilla attacks continued, decreasing in the late autumn each year when snowfall made movement in the mountainous south-east more difficult, and restarting the following spring.

In order to contain this new and serious challenge, the authorities resorted to a number of draconian measures to curb PKK insurgency. They embarked upon mass arrests following any guerrilla incident. The people of south-eastern Anatolia had been fearful of Turkey's armed forces ever since the establishment of the Republic, but a new phase of terror now began. Mass arrests took place, and beatings and torture became a commonplace experience among the Kurdish population. Whole villages would be surrounded and the menfolk carried off for interrogation. Physical and mental torture was routinely used on detainees. So fearful did the population become that some small children instinctively raised their hands above their heads when soldiers came to the village.

The authorities also took steps to seal the border areas with Syria and Turkey. In 1984 it was widely rumoured that they were considering the idea of creating a 20 km 'free-fire zone' by the forcible evacuation of villages within this belt but that, fearing international condemnation, they resorted to harassment instead, in the hope that the inhabitants would evacuate their villages. In addition fencing and minefields were established along the frontiers with Syria and Iraq. Although these measures inhibited movement, it seemed impossible to prevent completely.

Ankara therefore also negotiated an agreement on the 'hot pursuit' of guerrillas into Iraq. In May 1983 a major offensive against Kurdish positions just over the border in Iraq, using helicopter gunships to support ground troops, produced 2000 captives, most of whom turned out to be civilians. After a particularly successful attack on the gendarmerie post at Uludere in July 1986, Turkish jets strafed Kurdish camps of the Iraqi Kurdistan Democratic Party (KDP) as well as those of the PKK. It seems as if the attack on the KDP was deliberate.[25] Another major incursion took place in March 1987 when Turkish jets strafed three camps in northern Iraq. While Ankara claimed these were PKK camps, the KDP reported that it was Iraqi Kurds who were killed.[26]

'Hot pursuit' suited both Turkey and Iraq. The latter, heavily committed in its war against Iran, could ill-afford troop deployments along its northern border. Ankara, as the KDP quickly discovered, did not take much care in distinguishing between PKK or KDP guerrillas. Ankara and Baghdad shared a common interest in hitting all rebel Kurds hard.

Only two months after the 1983 incursion, the PKK had signed a co-operation agreement with the KDP in which each undertook to take no action which would damage the other. At the end of 1987 the KDP broke with the PKK, not only as a result of Turkish air strikes but more fundamentally over unease with the PKK's violent methods.

The PKK created ambivalent feelings among Turkey's Kurds. Its extreme leftist ideology worried traditionalist villagers. Its deliberate attacks on the 'accomplices' of the state, namely the large Kurdish landlords and aghas whose interests coincided with those of Ankara, shocked people by their brutality and ferocity, for in some cases whole families were massacred, regardless of sex or age. For example, in mid-July 1987 PKK fighters attacked the village of Pinarcik, killing 31 people, 19 of whom were children.[27] PKK fighters would call on villages in remote areas and compel threaten the inhabitants to provide food, shelter and information concerning troop movements.

Villagers found themselves in a dilemma, threatened with brutal retribution by each side if they co-operated with the other. As a result the conflict provoked much antagonism among the population. Nevertheless, Ankara was unlikely to win the competition for the hearts and minds of the population unless it adopted more sympathetic methods. But this it seemed unable to do. No sooner had Ankara (after eight years) lifted martial law in four south-eastern provinces than the eight predominantly Kurdish provinces of south-eastern Anatolia were placed under a governor- general in July 1987, with martial-law powers.[28] This governor-general was given sweeping powers, including control over all security forces operating in the region, the power to evacuate villages or pasture lands at his discretion, and supervision of civil trial procedure initiated against the security forces.

In effect, it added up to the suspension of civil rule and the reintro-duction of martial law.[29] A fact-finding mission by the Social Democrat Populist Party (SHP), the main opposition party, had already reported in 1986 that all of eastern Turkey had become a sort of concentration camp where every citizen was treated as a suspect, and where oppres-sion, torture and insult by the military was the rule;[30] such findings were confirmed by Amnesty International.[31]

For the civilian population, living in economically distressed cir-cumstances, subservient to autocratic landlords, and without prospects for the future, it was inevitable that troop brutality would create a con-stant stream of unemployed young recruits into the PKK. By the end of the decade, the ranks of the PKK were filled not only by young men but also by a considerable number of young women, marking a new social development within the nationalist forces.

It would be wrong, however, to conclude that the Kurdish popula-tion was unanimous in supporting the efforts of the PKK. Substantial numbers of Kurds, probably over 50%, remained either neutral or hos-tile to its activities. It was not difficult for the government to co-opt Kurdish landlords to raise local 'village guard' militias, from 1984 onwards. These enjoyed much the same freedom from the law as the Hamidiya chiefs almost a century earlier. In order to raise these guards, the government deliberately played on inter-family feuds in different localities, just as regimes in Baghdad had done for years. As a result, in many places it was well known that one leading family was 'pro-gov-ernment' while another was sympathetic to the PKK, new labels for longer-standing local struggles. These were often used to settle scores against rivals, or harass vulnerable groups.[32] By 1990 there were an esti-mated 24,000 members of the village guard system.

In some cases, villagers were coerced into joining the militia; and in others, villagers who refused to join were forcibly resettled.[33] Coercion became the currency of this savage brush-fire war. PKK intimidation even extended to press-gang techniques in order to obtain young recruits.[34]

Further tensions and refugee exodus: 1988-1990

The year 1988 was an important one in the Kurdish struggle inside Turkey. PKK insurgency widened, and casualty figures increased.[35] The PKK launched punitive raids on villages in retaliation, killing 27 vil-lagers. Whole families were gunned down.[36] It managed to rebuild rela-tions with Iraqi Kurds through an alliance with Jalal Talabani's Patriotic Union of Kurdistan (PUK) in May 1988.[37] It also began forging alliances with extreme leftist Turkish groups, most notably *Dev Sol* (Revolutionary Left). Yet by the end of 1988 the PKK had decided to abandon its attacks on civilian targets.

The government took counter-measures. In February Prime Minister Turgat Özal had sought Iranian co-operation in curbing border incursions, an official admission that PKK crossings were made not only on Turkey's southern borders but also from the east. The same month, gendarmes were replaced by regular troops along the Syrian and Iraqi borders.[38] In June the government promulgated Decree 285, permitting the deportation of people from the region at the discretion of the Regional Governor. Meanwhile a leading Turkish journalist who had interviewed the PKK leader, Abdallah Ocalan, in Lebanon, found himself charged under Articles 142 and 143 of the Penal Code on the serious offence of 'weakening national feelings'.[39]

Growing tension on the Kurdish question was also evident outside the government. The Social Democrat Populist Party was factionalized by the Kurdish question, with some deputies adhering to the Kemalist tradition, but others, particularly those from eastern Turkey, calling for greater sympathy for Kurdish autonomy.[40] In the second half of 1988 casualty figures reached new levels, with over 300 fighters, security forces and civilians killed in a three-month period.[41]

The sudden defeat of the Iraqi Kurds in August 1988 presented a difficult challenge for Turkey, since approximately 60,000 sought refuge inside the areas in which the PKK was operating. Ankara had no wish to fuel Kurdish national sentiment by permitting any contact with Iraqi Kurdish nationalists. There had, it is true, already been the first signs of greater openness when Kurdish Deputies in the National Assembly had called for some acceptance of the reality of Kurdish language and culture.[42] But popular Turkish feeling remained adamantly hostile to any concessions to its Kurds.

On the other hand, Turgut Özal was anxious to generate sufficient goodwill among the large Kurdish segment of Turkey's population to increase support for himself.[43] In the longer term, Özal's prospects of reducing Kemalist influence in the armed forces depended on his winning over the Kurdish population. With regard to Turkey's foreign relations also, Özal knew that the prospects for Turkey's entry into the European Community (EC) was partly contingent on an improved human rights record, particularly regarding the Kurds. Here was an opportunity to demonstrate the Republic's humanitarian character. Besides, the only means to prevent the entry of refugees from Saddam's gas attacks was by shooting those who attempted to cross the border – a course that would damage Turkey's relations with its NATO allies.

In fact, the government handled the refugee crisis with skill. It erected tented camps for the refugees and allowed foreign journalists to see for themselves its care and concern. But it was careful to allow no foreign aid workers into the camps, and refused to acknowledge the Kurdish fugitives as refugees.[44] It insisted on direct and sole control of the Kurds through the Turkish Red Crescent, calling for material and financial assistance to help cope with the problem. Many of the refugees were survivors of gas attacks, but Turkey quickly refused to comment on this, denying any conclusive physical evidence of chemical warfare among the refugees. Its motive seemed clear. It had already upset Iraq by allowing refugees, including pesh mergas, across the border, but was anxious to participate in Iraq's increased trade and forthcoming major reconstruction programme, expected to total $US 50,000 million in contracts.

Once international interest began to subside, in late September, Turkey took a number of steps to reduce and contain the Iraqi Kurdish issue. It secured an agreement in principle that Iran would receive some of these refugees, but unilaterally drove some 20,000 refugees across the border before Iran could halt the process. The remaining refugees – about 35,000 in number – it moved away from the border area to low-cost and unheated housing in Diyarbekir and Mush, and to a tented site near Mardin. It applied strict controls to prevent further refugee movement out of the camps, and to prevent further access by journalists or humanitarian workers. The rigours of the Anatolian winter were particularly hard for the very old and very young, with increased mortality and morbidity rates.

It seemed as if Turkey had come through the refugee dilemma relatively unscathed. But there can be little doubt that the refugee presence did affect local Kurdish sentiment. Many Turkish Kurds felt it their duty to help the refugees (some of whom, of course, were cousins) and the sight of Iraqi Kurds in Diyarbekir, in their distinctive costume, remained a daily reminder of Kurdish identity.

In 1989 the struggle continued to intensify. In January soldiers in Cizre Province indiscriminately rounded up Kurdish villagers, forced them to lie on the ground and stamped on them. Some villagers were reportedly forced to eat excrement. As *The Independent* reported:

> 'The alleged inhumanity meted out to villages in Cizre is not exceptional, according to members of the main opposition party, the Social Democrat (Populist) Party: since the beginning of January hundreds of peasants have been rounded up in similar campaigns to uncover supposed PKK supporters... Western diplomats here [Ankara] believe that

army brutality is widespread in the south-east. "What happened in Cizre comes as no surprise," said one. "There have been many reports of similar occurrences, though this is the worst to my knowledge."[45]

A week later, the Turkish weekly *Ikibine Dogru* alleged the existence of a mass grave after human remains were found under a refuse tip on the banks of Butcher's River, just outside the town of Siirt. It listed 67 missing Kurds believed to be in this grave, although at least 300 detained Kurds are unaccounted for. A government enquiry was inconclusive. It is unlikely the government would have made what would have been an acutely embarrassing admission in this regard. Two futher mass graves were reported in June 1989.[46] In mid-September the killing of six civilians by security forces resulted in a large protest demonstration in Silopi, in which reporters from leading Turkish papers were beaten up by police. The events were widely reported in the Turkish national press.

The Kurdish question was rapidly becoming the major domestic political issue. In October 1989 a major international symposium on the Kurdish question was convened in Paris. Seven Kurdish deputies belonging to SHP attended, and were immediately expelled from the party on their return to Turkey. Only their parliamentary immunity protected them from prosecution.[47] Their expulsion precipitated a number of resignations, at both central and regional levels in the party. Many of those who left the SHP formed a new political party, the People's Labour Party (HEP).[48] Even inside the ruling ANAP (Motherland) Party, similar tensions began to grow between a minority of more liberal party members who believed the Kurdish question had to be faced, and the majority who wished to deny the issue of any discussion.

6

THE KURDS IN TURKEY
– THE 1990S AND BEYOND

Yet it was in 1990 that the Kurdish question became Turkey's prime domestic concern. Scores were reported killed in the PKK's spring offensive. Forty-four schools were burnt down.[49] In March, however, a series of popular demonstrations broke out, most notably in Nusaybin and Cizre, where troops fired on the crowd, killing four civilians. These demonstrations occurred during the funeral of PKK fighters. In the past families had been frightened to claim such corpses, but now they began to demonstrate their pride in having a martyr in the family. Security forces imposed a curfew on 11 towns in Mardin and Siirt Provinces. The PKK soon described these disturbances as a Kurdish *intifada*, exaggerating their political importance. No sustained popular resistance along the lines of the Palestinian uprising followed.

With the security situation deteriorating, the government introduced draconian new measures in April 1990. Decree (*Kararname*) No 413 gave the Regional Governor of the Kurdish region sweeping powers: to recommend to the Minister of the Interior the closure of any publishing house that 'falsely reflects events in the region or engages in untruthful reporting or commentary'; forcibly to resettle 'those persons whom it is deemed necessary... in places which the Ministry of the Interior shall determine'.[50] Furthermore, those using the powers granted them by this decree were given immunity from prosecution. The decree provoked dismay in a wide spectrum of the Turkish press. When the SHP made an application against the decree in the Constitutional Court, the government redrafted and combined it with another one, renumbered as Decree No 424.[51]

The security forces used the new decree immediately, to muzzle press reporting and forcibly to remove thousands of villagers in the most seriously affected areas of Hakkari, Botan, Van and Siirt provinces.[52] In the mountains, special forces proved adept at tracking guerrilla groups and destroying them. Those captured were largely inexperienced fighters, suggesting that the PKK's veterans had already been killed or captured. Nevertheless the PKK suffered no shortage of recruits. The apparent ease with which the security forces were able to ambush groups in part reflected the fact that the PKK was swamped with new recruits which it was unable to train adequately.

However, while the security forces won the battle on the mountain, they were losing the struggle for hearts and minds in the towns and villages. Kurdish national feeling continued to advance. As in 1990 there were a number of clashes between civilian demonstrators and the security forces in Sirnak, Idil, Cizre, Midyat and elsewhere in early March 1991, and more demonstrations at *Now Ruz* (New Year) on 21 March, not only in Kurdistan but also in Adana, Izmir and Istanbul.[53] In July 1991 a string of assassinations of prominent Kurds culminated in the killing of the local chairman of the People's Labour Party (HEP), presumably by anti-Kurdish rightists. The following day security forces killed three and injured over one hundred, out of an estimated 20,000 protesters on the streets of Diyarbekir.

National feeling was also accelerated by the refugee crisis on the Turkish border at the end of March and popular disgust at the government's refusal to act humanely. Much of the aid extended by Turkey in fact came from fellow Kurds in the south-east.

Furthermore, in 1991 the PKK acted with renewed military vigour, ambushing security forces in villages and on roads close to towns. It seemed that the deliberate official depopulation programme in guerrilla areas was proving counterproductive, spreading the separatist contagion rather than containing it. Wherever disaffected civilians were resettled, the PKK knew it could hope for food, shelter or the provision of information concerning troop movements.

Saddam Hussein's occupation of Kuwait on 2 August 1990 created major problems for Turkey with regard to its own Kurds. Turkish co-operation with the United States was conditional on the understanding that in the event of the collapse of Iraq, no independent Kurdish entity would emerge in northern Iraq. It also reawoke old proprietorial feelings concerning the vilayet of Mosul.

Domestic and international pressures have created some movement in state behaviour towards the Kurds. In February a draft bill was presented to the National Assembly proposing to lift some of the restrictions on the Kurdish language. It was primarily Turgut Özal's idea, and provoked a storm of protest, not only from his own party but also from the SHP,[54] for departing from the Kemalist tradition. In fact the repeal of Law 2932 finally carried through in April 1991 permitted only Kurdish speech, song and music. It did not allow Kurdish to be used for political or educational purposes, or to be published or broadcast.

At the same time as this minimal concession, however, a new draconian Anti-Terror law was passed on 12 April defining terrorism as: 'any kind of action... with the aim of changing the characteristics of the Republic...', a definition which embraced any democratic attempt to moderate the stringent character of the State.[55]

A month earlier Özal had casually revealed that he had met Iraqi Kurdish leaders – at a moment when it seemed likely that the Kurds would break free from Baghdad's authority. This, too, provoked a storm of protest, since it broke another shibboleth of the state, that the Republic should not meddle in the internal affairs of a neighbour – least of all on behalf of Kurds. Yet by mid-1991 it was reliably rumoured that Özal had met leading army generals dismayed by his talks with Talabani, and had convinced them of the need to face the new political realities, however unpalatable they might seem.

In the meantime, the dramatic efforts by 400,000 Iraqi Kurds to find asylum in Turkey after the collapse of the uprising in Iraq at the end of March had given yet another turn of the screw to local Kurdish feeling. Turkish Kurds were disgusted by Ankara's behaviour, and did what they could to provide assistance themselves.

By mid-1991 the Turkish state seemed intent on increasing its security grip on the south-east, where approximately 2500 had died since 1984, while at the same time bowing to internal and external pressures to allow more debate on the Kurdish question. The question of Turkey's Kurds had become a greater domestic issue than ever before, and a growing number of Turks were increasingly critical regarding the efficacy of the old formula of repression and denial. Two themes were increasingly clear: oppression was proving counter-productive, but an alternative had yet to be found on which the political establishment could agree.

Specific factors

The development of Kurdish nationalism inside each state of the region has been distinctive. In Turkey's case there are specific factors which, even if they have also some relevance to the Kurdish situation elsewhere, are particularly acutely felt inside the Turkish Republic:

Underdevelopment characterizes Turkish Kurdistan. The average per-capita income is less than half the national average. Unemployment by the end of 1990 was estimated to be twice as high as the national average of 25%.[56] Economic deprivation is probably the single most important impetus to nationalism among ordinary Kurds. Unemployment, absence of prospects and a sense of grievance against the richer part of Turkey are major factors in nationalist feeling, quite apart from political discrimination against Kurds. Although considerable development has taken place in recent years, with the laying of metalled roads and the introduction of mechanized agriculture, the gap between it and western Anatolia remains wide. Furthermore, mechanization and better roads have accelerated unemployment and emigration, not reduced them.

The South-East Anatolia Development Project (GAP), which proposes the economic development of a large part of Turkish Kurdistan, is of doubtful value to the Kurds. Its 22 dams on the Tigris and Euphrates will supply Turkey with much of its energy (through hydro-electrity). They will also facilitate the introduction of irrigated and capital-intensive agriculture, most notably on the Harran plain. But who will benefit?

Land ownership patterns tell their own story. Eight per cent of farmers own over 50% of the farmland. Forty per cent of owner farmers are smallholders, with farms of less than five hectares in size, ie. on the very margins of viability. Many of these actually work their land under the supervision of, and sometimes in debt to, local large landowners. Another 40% are landless agricultural workers. The project proposes to co-ordinate the activities of smallholders on a co- operative basis. This is almost bound to result in the effective dispossession of the smallholders. Those who will benefit are the larger landholders who can afford the costs of fertilizers and machinery necessary to make a success of capital-intensive agriculture. The political establishment both in Ankara and in the provinces remains reluctant to introduce land reform (the last failed attempt was in 1978), because to do so would be to penalize the class which delivers the votes of much of the proletariat.

Education is another sector which betrays the failure of the state to address itself to the needs of the Kurds. The literacy rate in Mardin province is 48% compared with 77% nationally. Although primary education is compulsory, there is a heavy drop-out rate: only 18% of children commence the secondary cycle, and only 9% complete it.[57]

Far greater effort is necessary to attract the Kurdish population to education. Improvements to bring the quality of education up to the national standard are clearly important. But it is impossible to see how this can be done when children who speak Kurdish at home are required to learn in Turkish, even when they enrol in primary school. Until this politically motivated denial of Kurdish is removed, there can be little prospect of a significant improvement in educational standards in the south-east.

The second observation to be made is that so long as the Kurdish community remains uneducated, it will be unable to benefit from GAP. In other words, the economic regeneration of the south-east remains contingent on political liberalization, and the encouragement of the Kurdish people to express themselves freely in their own language.

Migration has been a major social experience. Well over a million Kurds moved westwards during the period 1950-80, and the flow continues. Some moved voluntarily in search of work, others moved because they were forced off the land by the introduction of mechanized farming. During the 1980s a large number moved as a result of either state harassment, or eviction, or destruction of their habitat by state security forces. It is significant that in the first two months of the Gulf crisis, August and September 1990, 27 villages and over 80 hamlets were evacuated and either mined or razed by government forces.[58]

Out of the total Kurdish population in Turkey of approximately 11 million, at least three million live in Istanbul and other Turkish cities. In fact, Istanbul is the largest Kurdish city anywhere. This seemingly innocent fact is of great significance for the protagonists. Although the PKK may draw the majority of its recruits from harassed villages, urban-based Kurds have been central to the advancement of political ideology. They have seen for themselves the disparity of economic standards between western and eastern Turkey. Although many Kurds seek to integrate and get on with making a living in a Turkish city, a minority become more politicized by their experiences uprooted from their cultural environment.

The Kurdish question has spread across Turkey. The state's counter-insurgency operation, particularly the evacuation of villages, is likely merely to spread the problem of separatism further. The PKK's call for an independent Kurdish state begs the question of the economic dependence of many Kurds, either seasonal workers or permanent workers outside Kurdistan.

Further afield, there are over 400,000 Turkish Kurds living in western Europe, mainly in Germany. Most came as guest workers. As for many Kurds in western Turkey, the experience has been a politicizing one, and the freedom and encouragement of political expression has inevitably afforded a vital impetus to Kurdish political thinking. Kurdish political groups and organizations exist in most European Community countries, and have helped develop the political ideologies which now inspire the various Kurdish parties in eastern Anatolia.

Migration inevitably also brings about a clash of cultures. Some are attracted by modern urban ideologies and cultures, others repelled. Returning to the village is not always easy, as one returnee after military service experienced:

'After the military, I went back home to my family's village (Kozluk), where my father was a big landowner. I worked for a Turkish newspaper in Batman, writing on the Kurdish question, against capitalism and against my own family. When I tried to help people in my village, my family called me "un-Muslim" because I tried to tamper with the God-given order of rich and poor.'[59]

7

THE ALEVI KURDS
– A MINORITY WITHIN A MINORITY

There are over three million Alevis[60] in east and south-eastern Turkey, of whom over one third are Kurds. The remainder are Turkish. Alevis are, broadly speaking, on the outer fringes of Shi'ite Islam. They live mainly in the mixed area where the Kurdish part of Turkey overlaps with the predominantly Turkish area. Kurdish Alevis are therefore a minority group within the totality of Alevis. They are also usually an ethnic minority in the districts where they are to be found, the majority being Turkish. Among the Kurdish community also, they are a minority as the vast majority of Turkey's Kurds (about 85%) are Sunni Muslim. Virtually all those seeking asylum in Britain during May and June 1989 were both Kurdish *and* Alevi.

If, as was suggested by the Home Secretary at the time, these asylum-seekers or a substantial proportion of them, were essentially 'economic refugees' (itself a contradiction in terms), one must ask why Turks did not come (since these are not only the vast majority of Turkey's citizens, but a majority in the areas from which these asylum-seekers came), and why Sunni Muslim Kurds did not come either, since these also live in some of the areas from which these asylum-seekers came. The answers to these questions are complex, but essential to understanding why Alevi Kurds have felt compelled to leave their homes in east and south-eastern Turkey.

Alevi beliefs

There are specific historical, religious and political reasons why Alevis are subject to harassment. The term 'Alevi' is sometimes used in a general sense to denote a wide variety of Shi'i and dervish sects, but it is used more specifically to describe the mixture of Shi'i Islam, Persian Mazdeism, Christianity and possibly central Asian ideas adopted by the Turkoman and Kurdish tribes who inhabited parts of eastern Anatolia at the beginning of the 16th Century, before the Ottomans had extended their control to the area.

These Alevis, known more frequently as *'Kizilbash'* ('Red Heads', on account of their distinctive turbans), supported the Shi'i Persian Empire against the Sunni Ottomans. When the Ottomans successfully drove the Persian forces out of eastern Anatolia in 1514, the Alevis were unwillingly incorporated into the Ottoman Empire. At the time, an estimated 40,000 Alevis were killed by the victorious Ottomans.

Alevis have been treated with contempt ever since, on account of their political and religious dissidence from the Ottoman Sunni establishment. Sunni Muslims have always derided Alevis as 'extinguishers of light', alleging nocturnal orgies – a defamatory and falsifying folklore akin to that which persisted concerning Jews in many parts of Europe. The very term 'Kizilbash', which was once an acceptable nomenclature, is now considered by Alevis to be defamatory.[61]

Although by their title ('followers of Ali'), the Alevis claim to be within the framework of Islam, their system of beliefs are unrecognisable as such to Sunni Muslims. They do not observe any of the five fundamental requirements of Islam: the *shahada* (statement of faith); the performance of prayer five times daily; almsgiving; fasting in Ramadan; the *Hajj* (the pilgrimage to Mecca). Of particular repugnance to Sunni Muslims is the Alevi failure to observe the cleansing rituals necessary for Sunnis before prayer. Alevis are thus considered a pollutant in the community.

Alevis insist that it is the condition of the heart and mind which is important, not the outward rituals. Alevi villages are distinguishable by the absence of mosques (unless government authorities have inflicted one on the village), and by the fact that Alevi women usually go unveiled. Trees in Alevi areas are frequently the object of veneration, particularly if they are close to the tomb of a holy man, and may often be found with votive rags tied to the branches.

Alevi life

Alevis, like many other deviant sects, sometimes practice dissimulation (*taqiya*) in order to avoid discrimination or persecution. Taqiya is an accepted practice among Shi'i and extreme Shi'i sects as a mode of survival in a hostile Sunni world. In the Alevi context, taqiya is a good deal easier for Turks, who share the same mother tongue as the Sunni Muslim majority. Kurds usually give themselves away by their accent, and if they come from the Alevi area they are assumed to be Alevi. Many Kurdish Alevis do not even speak the main Kurdish dialect, Kurmanci, but speak (along with some Turkish Alevis) a local dialect,

Zaza. (Confusingly, quite a few Sunnis, both Turkish and Kurdish, also speak Zaza). A few male Alevi Kurds apparently remain uncircumcised[62] and are liable to discovery during military service.

The Alevis generally, and Kurdish Alevis in particular, are identified with the left in Turkish politics. One reason may be that in the face of Sunni discrimination many (even secularized) Alevis have explored the cultural dimension of their particularism in the strong tradition of songs and poetry by Pir Sultan Abdal, a 16th Century mystic and social rebel executed by the authorities. Alevis see a link between his ideas of social justice and the modern struggle of the Alevi community. The relatively democratic socio-economic system of Alevi villages (most tend not to be subject to large landlords, but to hold equitable portions of village land and work these co-operatively) and Alevi underclass status also incline them towards the political left in modern Turkish politics.[63]

A number of Turkish Alevis claim a Kurdish identity. Some embraced Kurdish culture centuries ago (they speak Kurdish but sing old Turkoman songs), at a time when some nomadic Sunni Kurdish tribes intermingled with Turkoman Alevi ones, the former adopting the Alevi system of beliefs, the latter adopting Kurdish culture. Other Turks very recently adopted Kurdish identity as a symbol of their underclass and rejected status.

Kurdish Alevis are largely village people, living in inhospitable mountain areas of Dersim (renamed by the authorities as Tunceli) or in malarial marsh areas near Marash which they themselves laboriously drained. With population growth, some have drifted to the predominantly Sunni Muslim towns of the area, where they have tended to live in their own slum quarters. Thus they remain visibly marginalized.

Political persecution

In the 1970s some Alevis were active politically, and as a result the community as a whole became the target of rightist reprisals during the disorders of the late 1970s. In 1967, 40 or so Alevis from Sivas were set upon and killed during a football match in Kayseri. In 1978 tensions between the rightists and leftists in Marash province culminated in a major massacre of Alevis organized by the fascist Grey Wolves (National Action Party), in which at least one hundred, and probably several hundred, died.

In the 1980s the mood changed from a left-right political confrontation (the Grey Wolves have fallen into abeyance) to a religious one, between Sunni-Muslim revivalists (attracting many of the old rightists) and those who are either heretical (ie. Alevis) or are secularists (thus including many of those who upheld a leftist viewpoint in the 1970s). Some Sunni revivalists are quite candid in saying that Alevis are little better than animals and that it is acceptable or even meritorious for Muslims to kill them. These revivalists did particularly well in the Marash area in the 1989 local elections, and one of those elected to the Marash council was Okkes Kengar, a rightist closely identified with the 1978 massacre. Alevis feel it is 'open season' against them, and are understandably terrified by the success of such people.

The recent rise of Muslim fundamentalism in the area (and the harassment of Alevis which this implies), and particularly the result of the March 1989 local elections, almost certainly accounts for the sudden flight of so many Kurdish Alevis in May and June 1989. Unsubstantiated rumours also suggest that fear was deliberately fostered by unscrupulous racketeers who offered to get Kurdish Alevis to Britain and to find them employment.

It might be thought that the government could take action against Muslim fundamentalism which, after all, is inimical to the Ataturk legacy. Officially, the government is secular but Sunni Islam remains perceived as the established religion, and there is a culture of hostility to Shi'ism and more particularly to Alevis.

The Turkish Prime Minister is himself religious and has ties with the Naqshbandi religious order, which in Turkey is closely associated with the Islamic revival. Furthermore, his Motherland Party is increasingly dependent on the support of Muslim revivalist parties as its own constituency has been severely weakened. Turkey's NATO allies will not wish to embarrass the Turkish government on this issue, and are therefore tempted to play down Turkey's human rights record, particularly with regard to the Kurds.

It is at the local level that the tone of persecution is set. The crude form is the widespread arbitrary arrests and torture mentioned above, to which Alevis are more subject than Sunni Muslim Kurds. Many asylum-seekers have become a target of harassment on account of a relative's political activities.

In the 1970s the army was more sympathetic to the rightists than the leftists. Today it turns a blind eye to Sunni Muslim harassment of Kurdish Alevis, or actually joins in. It is neither purely Turkish persecution of Kurds, nor purely Sunni persecution of Alevis which is going on, but rather a combination of the two, whereby Kurdish Alevis have good reason to claim they are persecuted.

At an everyday level, in addition to the suppression of linguistic and cultural identity and the arbitrary harassment, arrest and torture suffered at the hands of the authorities, Kurdish Alevi villages often do not receive services offered to Turkish Sunni villages . For example, the village inhabitants are told to build a mosque (and to pray in it) if they wish to receive their entitlement, eg to have a secondary school or a road laid. If an Alevi Kurdish trader, to quote another example given by several asylum-seekers, has his stall deliberately ransacked, any complaint will probably result in his alos getting a beating from the police. The authorities send Sunni Muslim teachers to primary schools in Alevi Kurdish villages where, Alevis claim, they indoctrinate the children with Islam and act as informers in the village.

Eating or smoking during daylight hours in Ramadan is likely to provoke physical assault, even if done at home. Alevi Kurds discover it is safer to suffer in silence. Even if they go somewhere like Istanbul, they face neighbourhood hostility. They must be extremely careful in their behaviour. Like Jews in Tsarist Russia, Alevi Kurds have become used to abuse and harassment – but by 1989 many felt themselves at breaking point.

In addition to harassment by the Sunni populace, the security forces routinely harass Alevis in pursuit of members of illegal organizations. In the words of one Alevi Kurdish asylum-seeker:

> 'At first they [the police] started calling at 2 or 3 am, kicking the door in and coming inside to look for Yusuf. They would threaten me and the family. They would ask me where he was and shout at me, calling me a Kurdish communist. They told me that if I would not talk they would take my wife and children. They said they would rape my wife [Amnesty International reports a number of cases of rape in detention]. We had children and all this was shouted in front of them.'

Such an account is not isolated. Routine harassment and police terror are such that, in the words of another asylum-seeker:

> 'The children had become so fearful that whenever a policeman came to the house they would immediately put their hands on their heads as a gesture of surrender.'[64]

The role of the state

The Kurdish Alevis, located in the marginal area between predominantly Kurdish and Turkish regions, live in areas where many resettlement and afforestation schemes are under way. Forced resettlement fulfils both economic and political objectives. Large parts of eastern and south-eastern Turkey have been designated either for commercial afforestation or for agricultural development as part of regional development plans. It is possible that millions may be forcibly relocated, usefully reducing the Kurdish population in areas of PKK activity.

Tunceli has been an area of considerable PKK activity, and consequently a target for state repression. It was primarily Alevi Kurds who fought against the government so bitterly in 1938. Martin van Bruinessen, a leading European authority on Kurdistan, writes:

> 'The province of Tunceli, always a hotbed of political dissent, was characterized as "Turkey's largest prison"... Turkish attempts to break the backbone of Kurdish nationalism and of the PKK in particular have consisted of more forced assimilation, close and brutal police surveillance, and massive resettlement. Many families, sometime entire villages, have been deported from districts where PKK have been active.'[65]

While the government has denied that relocation is forced, there is evidence that it is. One circular from the Director-General of Forestry, for example, says that 'those villagers who do not apply (for relocation assistance) should be made aware... that they will be transferred'.[66] In Tunceli region, out of 414 listed villages, only 134 either have forests or have been designated for afforestation. Nevertheless, 355 villages have been told to prepare for resettlement under the Afforestation Law. In Erzincan, further east, only 29 villages either have forest or are designated for afforestation. Nevertheless, 250 villages have been told to prepare for resettlement.[67]

There have been reports of Alevi Kurds having their land seized at gunpoint by Sunni Kurds, in some cases belonging to the pro-government Village Guards. Courts have apparently failed to reinstate Alevi titleholders, either as a result of intimidation or because of the close ties between Kurdish landlords and local government.[68]

Compensation, either in cash or in land, seems to depend upon qualifying as a loyal citizen of the state. It is reported from the area south of Marash, for example, that only those known to be neither militants nor sympathizers with Kurdish separatism, and to be literate in Turkish, will receive a grant of alternative land. Such stipulations effectively disqualify many Kurdish citizens from any form of compensation. It is difficult not to conclude that such measures are deliberately aimed as marginalizing the Kurdish community.

Thus there are political, religious, economic and social dimensions to the persecution Alevi Kurds suffer, but it is misrepresenting the nature of persecution to suggest that these asylum-seekers are economic migrants, even where they are victims of land expropriation. Those returned to Turkey face many risks, ranging from daily harassment, through economic dispossession, cultural or religious harassment to torture and killing. No one can be sure that, because he has not himself directly suffered the most brutal end of the spectrum, he will not do so if he is returned. Even seeking asylum is evidence of 'disloyalty' to the state.

Some of those returned against their will have been lucky to re-enter Turkey unnoticed, but others have been detained and beaten on re-entry.[69] In the words of one returnee trying to leave Istanbul airport:

> *'A policeman came up behind me and grabbed hold of my arm. He took me up to the second floor to a room there. As soon as we got in he started slapping me across the face and kicking me. He accused me of being a traitor. He said, "Wherever you go, you will be back here!" He called me a dirty Kurd. He then locked me up..."*[70]

The adverse circumstances currently faced by Alevi Kurds in their own country are likely to persist until the Turkish state takes effective measures to deter persecution by the army, local authorities and by aggressive Sunni Muslims.

8

THE KURDS IN IRAN
– UNDER THE SHAHS

Kurdish relations with the government of Iran have not been much better than those with the Turkish government, although Iran has never exercised quite the same level of implacable brutality. It has been unable to since, unlike Turkey which apart from its Kurds is relatively homogeneous, Iran has substantial Arab, Turkic, and Baluchi minorities in addition to the Kurds. Kurds have more in common with Iranians in language and cultural affinity than with either Turks or Arabs. This sense of affinity impels today's Kurds towards autonomy within Iran rather than independence from it.

Rule by the Safavids

After the defeat at Chaldiran in 1514, the Safavid shahs tried to consolidate power in their empire by direct rule, but subsequently recognized non-tribal paramount families controlling two or three main confederations. They used Kurdish tribes to defend the border in Khorasan against Uzbeg invaders in 1600 and these became a permanent community over the years.

As their predecessors had done, the Safavids dealt ruthlessly with recalcitrant Kurdish princes, but never achieved the effective arrangement of self-rule negotiated by the Ottomans with their Kurdish princes. This must be partly explained by the fact that most of the Kurdish tribes were Sunni, and therefore less amenable to defending the frontier of a Shi'i empire. It was also because, living in close proximity to two strong states, the ruling families frequently split into pro-Ottoman and pro-Iranian branches. Frontier tribes and emirates vacillated between recognition of Safavid and of Ottoman authority.

Subsequently the rise of pro-Russian and pro-British factions in the great ruling families reflected the growth of imperial influence in the region in the 19th Century when, like the Ottomans, the Qajar Shahs decided to replace Kurdish princely governors with direct administration. The last and greatest of the Iranian Kurdish princes, of Ardelan, was finally deprived of his power in 1865. Despite the treatment they received from the Shahs, Kurdish chiefs demonstrated their commitment to the old order by supporting the Qajar attempt to overthrow the constitutional government of 1912.

Like Turkey at the end of World War I, Iran was also plunged into internal turmoil. Reza Khan, founder of the Pahlavi dynasty, managed with fortunate outside circumstances and British encouragement to establish himself as effective ruler in Tehran in 1921, although he did not displace the last of the Qajar Shahs until 1923, and did not proclaim himself Shah until 1925. His overriding concern in his first years was to ensure the integrity of a state composed of different groups, Kurds, Azeri Turks, Arabs in Khuzistan, Lurs, Bakhtiars and others. Successful separatism on the part of any one of these communities could prove fatal to the integrity of the rest.

Amongst several separatist risings in different parts of post-World War I Iran, by far the most serious was that in Kurdistan. In October 1921 a Kurdish chief, Isma'il Shakkak Simko, threw off government authority in the area west and south of Lake Urmiya. At first the government in Tehran tried to reach agreement with Simko on the basis of limited Kurdish autonomy. When Simko incited Lur tribes to join his revolt, and occupied Maraghah east of Lake Urmiya in 1922, Reza Khan led an expedition which dispersed his followers and drove him into Iraq.

Simko's revolt had almost certainly been a mix between personal aggrandizement and some kind of nationalism. It was also a good example of the way in which a Kurdish chief, surrounded by loyal and wholly ruthless retainers, could dramatically change the balance of things at a time of weakness and disorder.[71]

He first rose to prominence during the chaotic years of World War I when the Tehran government welcomed his attempt to provide authority in the sensitive region west of Urmiya at a time when it was threatened by Turkish, Russian and British forces. When he found himself in competition with Assyrian Christians, themselves trying equally ruthlessly to carve out an independent state near Urmiya, he had no scruple in eliminating them. They would have done the same.

Simko was a classic Kurd chief who, like those who joined the Hamidiya cavalry, used government recognition at a time of uncertainty to advance his own power. Neighbours had either to be eliminated or forced into alliance as subordinates. It was the way confederations were made and unmade. It is unlikely that Simko himself would have been able to distinguish personal ambition from nationalist sentiment. The rise of Mulla Mustafa Barzani in Iraq 40 years later was to reflect the same path – use of the government to reinforce his position locally, followed by a bid to throw off government control and establish his own independence.

Throughout the 1920s and 1930s Reza Khan suppressed separatist tendencies throughout Iran, amongst the Turkic tribes and the Arabs of Khuzistan as well as the Kurds. Lands were confiscated and sometimes whole tribes moved off their ancestral lands.

The Mahabad Republic

During World War II the Russians occupied northern Iran, and the British occupied the south. The objective was to dislodge Reza Shah who, the Allies suspected was likely to turn his pro-German sympathy into military alliance. A power vacuum resulted in the Kurdish area between the two zones, with some areas, Shahpur and Urmiya, falling under Soviet control. In the hope of using the opportunity to break loose from Iranian tutelage, Kurdish nationalists in 1942 formed a party, *Komala Jiwanewey Kurd* (The Kurd Resurrection Group).

Under Soviet influence but not control, both the Kurds and the Azerbaijani Turks further north were able to direct their own affairs. The Soviets still harboured an interest in annexing the Azerbaijan area which they had coveted throughout much of the 19th Century, and were also extremely interested in oil concessions in north Iran. But the Allies had, at the time of their invasion, also pledged themselves to withdraw from Iran by March 1946.

As that time drew near, the Kurds and Azerbaijanis formalized their independence from Tehran. In December 1945 Azerbaijanis captured Tabriz with Soviet encouragement, and declared a Democratic Republic of Azerbaijan. Following the Azerbaijani lead, the Kurds declared the Republic of Mahabad a few days later, and in January 1946 formed a government under the presidency of *Qazi* (judge) Muhammad, a respected member of a leading family of Mahabad.

The Republic was outside the area actually occupied by Soviet forces, stretching from Urmiya (Rezaiah) northwards, and was unable to incorporate Kurdish areas of Saqqiz, Sanandaj and Kermanshah to the south which were within the Anglo-American zone of control. It was thus pitifully small. The government was formed by the Kurdish Democratic Party (KDPI), an amalgam and compromise between older groups, *Komala*, Hiwa, a younger Iraqi leftist party, and a group of Kurdish communists.

The long-standing divisions between Kurds, even in so small an area, were soon apparent. Before the declaration of the republic, the Soviets had already encouraged separatism, not through leftist political groups, but more pragmatically through tribal chiefs.[72] Each of these had been evasive, reluctant to jeopardize his own pivotal position between government and tribespeople. Following the declaration of the republic, many other lesser chiefs in the area had avoided becoming too closely involved with the Mahabad regime, which found itself dependent mainly on relatives of the locally popular Qazi Muhammad and other citizens of Mahabad. Only the fortuitous acquisition of Mulla Mustafa Barzani (in flight from the British and Hashemites in Iraq) and 3000 followers in November 1945 made the republic's position defendable.

Whether or not the Mahabad Republic was set upon a path to complete independence is questionable. At the time of its establishment it sought complete autonomy *within* Iran's frontiers. Within the republic Kurdish became the official language, periodicals appeared, and the economy benefited from direct trade with the USSR. A number of traditional leaders had fled rather than be implicated in a movement which would destroy their own powerful position between Tehran and their tribal or village populations. The land of such chiefs was redistributed, but not on leftist principles. Some of it went to the Barzanis from Iraq. Leftists and traditionalists were anxious to compromise in order to keep the republic afloat.

At a political level the Mahabad Government expected the USSR to stand by them although, since pragmatism had led the Soviets to approach tribal leaders in spring 1945 rather than to sponsor ideologically correct republics, this was wishful thinking. The expectation also ignored widespread Kurdish suspicion of the Russians, based on Russian incursions into Azerbaijan in the 19th Century, and the way in which Russians had laid bare parts of Kurdistan, including sacking Mahabad during World War I.

Kurdish political groups elsewhere were hostile to Qazi Muhammad's Soviet connections. Tribes in the region suffered economically from Soviet occupation and from the Mahabad Republic, since they could not make their customary tobacco crop sales to other parts of Iran. West of Mahabad both the Mamesh and Mangur tribes (the closest tribes to the town) were bitterly hostile to Mahabad, to the extent that Barzani's men, who had outlasted their welcome in the area, were sent against them.

The Mahabad Government also badly miscalculated Soviet interests. Although the Soviets had encouraged both Azerbaijan and Mahabad to declare autonomous republics, they were not prepared to defend them. Regardless of whether either was a sound 'soviet' – and it was manifestly clear Mahabad was not – Soviet interests lay in its overall relationship with Iran, and with the oil exploration concession that it was not only interested in but managed to obtain (though it was subsequently not ratified by Iran's parliament) in spring 1946.

By late May 1946 the Soviets had left Iranian soil. Their military help to the Kurdish Republic did not extend beyond persuading a few petty tribal chiefs always ready for fighting and loot to join the Qazi and to comvince the reluctant Amr Khan of the Shikak (who had resigned from the Mahabad Government) to reaffirm his support. Despite honest attempts, Qazi Muhammad was unable to reach an agreement with Tehran. He was aware that a majority of Kurds under their tribal chiefs were unwilling to support him and liable to support the government.

In December 1946 the Iranian army advanced on Azerbaijan where the republic collapsed almost without resistance, some of its leadership fleeing to the USSR. Amr Khan once more changed sides, pledging loyalty to Tehran and, along with other chiefs, being accepted back into the fold. Soon afterwards Iranian troops entered Mahabad unopposed, with Kurdish tribesmen of the closest tribes to Mahabad (the Dehbokri, Mamesh and Mangur) in the van of the advancing column. Qazi Muhammad, a man of honour to the end, made no attempt to flee. Barzani withdrew with his men to the Iraqi side of the border.

All traces of Qazi Muhammad's regime were eradicated. The printing press was closed, the teaching of Kurdish prohibited, and the people of Mahabad burnt their Kurdish books. The area was disarmed, though those Kurdish tribes which had co-operated with the Iranian government were exempted. In March 1947 Qazi Muhammad and two of his colleagues were publicly hanged in Mahabad's main square. Eleven chiefs were also hanged to encourage loyalty amongst the others.

For the Kurds the episode of Mahabad held bitter lessons. Barely one third of the Iranian Kurds had fallen inside the Mahabad Republic. Many of these did not actively oppose but certainly did not support it. Much rested on the personal prestige of Qazi Muhammad within the town. Beyond the 'liberated zone' few Kurds demonstrated their willingness either to rebel where they were or to march to Mahabad's aid. Most stayed at home. Belief in, and dependence on, outside powerful sponsors was shown to be dangerous, potentially suicidal. The military strength of the Kurds still lay in the hands of tribal chiefs, and these proved to be quarrelsome, capricious, unreliable, and politically uncommitted to the same ideas as urban intellectuals and nationalists. The same bitter lessons were to be replayed in Iraq.

The post-war period

After the fall of Mahabad, as in Turkey after the fall of Dersim in 1938, the Kurdish nationalist movement went underground, and expression of Kurdish identity was banned. In 1952 when the Kurdish peasants of Bokan revolted against their landlords, the KDPI gave a lead. The Iranian army quickly came to the assistance of landowners, crushing any resistance. The KDPI met secretly in 1956, a full decade after Mahabad, and adopted a leftist programme.

Following the Iraqi Revolution of 1958, and the rehabilitation of Barzani in Iraq, Iranian Kurds became increasingly active politically, and increasingly harassed by the authorities. Two leading members of the KDPI Central Committee were arrested and remained in jail until the revolution of 1979. In 1959 at least 250 activists were arrested, whilst others escaped to Baghdad.

The Iranian Kurds remained heavily dependent upon Barzani and his movement in Iraq. Under his influence the KDPI produced a more conservative leadership. When KDPI organized a conference in Iraqi Kurdistan, some less 'conservative' delegates and many leftists were forcibly prevented from attending. Some KDPI cadres led limited guerrilla activity against the Iranian regime, which responded with harsh repression. Barzani, who was receiving aid from the Shah, blocked those in Baghdad from returning to Iran, and refused any help to those operating inside Iran. In 1968 he executed one of the leaders (Sulaiman Muini) and handed the corpse over to the Iranian authorities, who publicly displayed it in a number of Kurdish towns.

It was an unfortunate precedent in pan-Kurdish co-operation. The movement in Iran collapsed, many militants having to go into hiding, and more than 40 KDPI members were either killed or arrested by Barzani's men and handed over to the Iranians. Within Iran the Kurds were watched by the Shah's secret police, SAVAK, and by the army and gendarmerie. Some inevitably became paid informants for the regime, and fear and suspicion prevailed amongst all those with political views.

The agreement between Barzani and the Iraqi government in 1970 made Baghdad the centre of Iranian Kurdish activity. The KDPI (which had moved to the left in the meantime) adopted an anti-imperialist position, declaring their opposition to the Shah's regime. It enjoyed the enthusiastic backing of the Ba'th regime in Baghdad, which provided it with arms and money. At the very same time Barzani was still receiving large amounts of aid from the Shah, and he did not allow KDPI to translate Ba'thi support into any kind of initiative inside Iran. When Barzani broke with Baghdad, however, in 1974 KDPI refused to

1. Kurdish pesh mergas at a front-line position in the mountains of Iraqi Kurdistan, 1966. LORD KILBRACKEN

2. Pesh mergas in a secret mountain hide-out making grenades.
LORD KILBRACKEN

3. General Mustafa Barzani (1903-1979), the legendary Kurdish leader, photographed in 1969.

4. Iraqi gassing of Kurds at Halabja, April 1988

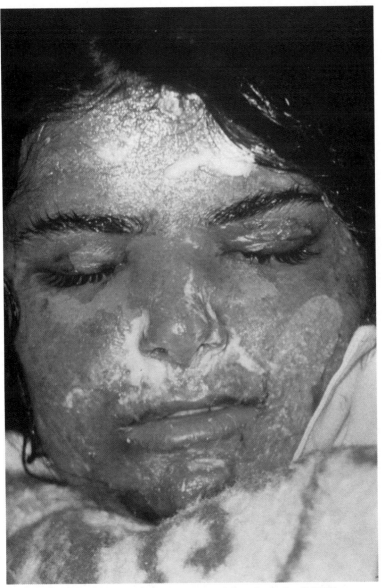

5. Child victim of chemical weapons, Halabja, Iraq, April 1988.

6. *Long live the brotherhood of Arabs and Kurds!* Kurdish demonstration in Moscow, 1988. INSTITUT KURDE DE PARIS

7. Refugees from Iraq queuing outside the HQ of the relief operation SAR. Dajht, Iran, April 1991. ADAM HINTON/SELECT

8. Iraqi soldiers captured by pesh mergas, March 1991.
DON MCCULLIN/MAGNUM

9. Kurdish refugees fleeing Northern Iraq, April 1991. BRUNO BARBEY/MAGNUM

10. British Red Cross aid, en route to Iran, for relief of the Kurdish refugees, April 1991.
DAVID STEWART-SMITH/INSIGHT

11. Kurdish pesh merga with captured Iraqi army weaponry, near Piranshahr, Iraq, April 1991. DAVID STEWART-SMITH/INSIGHT

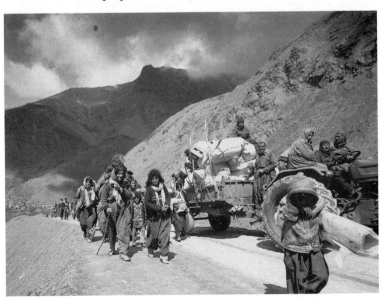

12. Refugees from Iraq walking into Iran near Sulaymaniyah, Iraq, April 1991. ADAM HINTON/SELECT

13. Refugees crossing the Iran-Iraq border near Sulaymaniyah, Iraq, April 1991. ADAM HINTON/SELECT

denounce Barzani publicly, and they were expelled from Iraq. In Iran, on the other hand, militant Kurds felt they could not attack the Shah's regime whilst it was supporting Barzani's struggle against Baghdad. They were caught in a double-bind.

When Iraq and Iran concluded their sudden and dramatic agreement in Algiers in March 1975 whereby the Shah undertook to withdraw support to Barzani, antagonism between Iranian Kurds and the regime in Tehran was resumed. But unlike Iraq, where the mainstream of Kurdish expression was through tribal loyalties exemplified by Barzani himself, the leader of KDPI since 1973 had been Abdul Rahman Ghassemlou, a socialist intellectual who had taught at the Sorbonne and lived for some years in Czechoslovakia, and the rank-and-file nationalists were peasants and townspeople. It welcomed active co-operation with other progressive forces determined to overthrow the Shah's regime. Although militarily weaker than the tribal army of Barzani, it promised a far better basis for national struggle.

9

THE KURDS IN IRAN
— UNDER THE ISLAMIC REPUBLIC

The Islamic revolution of 1979

The downfall of the Shah in January 1979 and the disintegration of the state apparatus provided an unrivalled opportunity for Kurdish demands for autonomy, far greater than that offered to the people of Mahabad, since Soviet or other Great Power interest or physical presence was not involved.

To back their demands the Kurds took over police and army barracks in the area from the erstwhile Shah's troops, acquiring a substantial amount of arms and ammunition. Since Ghassemlou had consistently advocated co-operation with other revolutionary groups, the Kurds had every reason to be optimistic.

Not all the Kurds were enthusiastic about the Shah's downfall. A powerful group of tribal chiefs, and their immediate followers, lost the financial and political rewards they had enjoyed in ensuring tranquillity in the area. The Jaf chiefs, for example, had been given high-level posts in local and central government, whilst their enormous landholdings were practically untouched by the Shah's land reform programme.[73] Sardar Jaf became an influential tribal member of the *majlis* (lower house of parliament) whilst his brother Salar Jaf was a high-level official in the Shah's palace. Likewise some of the Ardalan chiefs were prominent servants of the Shah, including the Court Minister up to the time of the Shah's downfall. One of the most loyal supporters of the Shah was the Kurdish Governor- General of Kermanshah, General Palizban, who continued to trouble the Islamic republic from a base in Iraq.

Other traditional leaders, however, took advantage of government weakness to assert their independence. Simko's son, Tahir Khan, raised the Shikak, Herki and other local tribes against gendarmerie posts, very reluctantly calling on the KDPI for assistance. As Tahir Khan must have recognized, this necessity elevated the KDPI in the eyes of tribesmen, undermining his own leadership. Later in the year he turned away from KDPI, joining other chiefs actively working against it. On the other hand, a number of Shikak sided with KDPI, and the latter intervened several times to arbitrate between chieftains trying to collect traditional dues and their peasantry. The struggle between tribal and party political organizations is far from resolved.

The revolutionary government in Tehran was virtually bound to reject Kurdish autonomist demands. Its mandate, and the revolutionary tide on which it had risen to power, was Islamic, and central to its beliefs was the unity of the Islamic community (*umma*), a concept more religious than secular in nuance, and therefore less negotiable. Self-administration perhaps, but autonomy never. The only minorities recognized in the new Islamic constitution were religious ones.

The dispute was also religious. Those Kurds who were Shi'i, in Kermanshah area, tended to support Khomeini in Tehran. Shaikh Izzedin Husaini, the Kurdish political and religious (Sunni) leader, opposed Khomeini's theological justification to power since its basis was the clergy's role of active participation in government rather than that of guides and interpreters of Islamic law to government. Later on, when the Kurds had broken completely with the government, he challenged their position accordingly:

> 'Many governments in the past have claimed to act in the name of Islam, but in reality they were not Islamic. The Safavid and Ottoman governments were cases in point; more recently we have the case of Khomeini in Iran. They are qeshri – reactionary and sectarian – and have ruined Islam and its spirit. What we have is not religious government, but a dictatorship under the name of Islam... In Sunni Islam there is no imam as political guide or na'ib [deputy]) imam. The role of the clergy is to be murshid, or guide, in knowing God. You will also find some Shi'i clergy who reject Khomeini's concept of faqih [jurisprudent]. It is not an Islamic regime.'[74]

From early 1979 until Iraq invaded Iran 18 months later, the Kurds and Tehran played out a struggle through negotiation and armed clashes. The Kurds were unwilling to let slip the chance for genuine autonomy. Tehran was unwilling to allow Kurdistan to slip from its control. Whilst reluctant to antagonize the Kurds, it also had to deal with the alarming phenomenon of creeping de facto autonomy. Islamic belief apart, if it ceded autonomy to the Kurds, then the Azerbaijanis, and the Arabs of Khuzistan, and the Baluchis in the south-east, might clamour for similar rights, and Iran could disintegrate.

Two Kurdish leaders emerged, Abdul Rahman Ghassemlou, the Secretary-General of KDPI, the primary political organization in Iranian Kurdistan, and the widely respected religious leader already mentioned, Shaikh Izzedin Husaini. He was able to exercise a unifying role as shaikh amongst the Kurdish population and enjoy more respect with the Shi'ite leadership in Tehran than could the KDPI and other leftists. Although he stressed that the Kurds were not separatists, the terms of autonomy were unacceptable in Tehran. When KDPI militants took over Mahabad barracks, and their Iraqi compatriots further antagonized the government by attacking Iranian police posts, the local Kurds, including KDPI and the extreme leftist *Komala* (Revolutionary Organization of the Kurdish Toilers), shrewdly used Shaikh Husaini to parley.

The government was uncertain whether it wished to placate or punish the Kurds. Ever since the fall of the Shah, there had been clashes between the *Pasdaran* (Revolutionary Guards) and Kurdish peasants backed by Komala and the Kurdish members of Fedayin Khalq, who were seizing land previously belonging to traditional landlords around Sanadaj and Merivan. Komala accused the regime of using Pasdaran, reactionary Kurds led by Shi'ite Ayatullah Safdari, feudal landlords and the Barzani forces against them. Throughout spring and summer the clashes between Kurds and government forces intensified, with accusations being hurled back and forth.

War against the Kurds

Major clashes in July 1979, when government troops sought to reoccupy a police post close to the Turkish border, and in August, when the government attempted to reassert its authority over Merivan, persuaded the government in favour of a military solution. On 16 August 1979 the Kurds had captured the town of Paveh. Two days later Khomeini assumed powers as commander-in-chief of the armed forces, and sent the army, with helicopter-gunships, phantom jets and tanks and artillery to attack and occupy Paveh, Sanandaj and Saqqiz.

The fall of these towns was a sharp reminder that the Iranian army was not in disarray, and that its defeat in conventional warfare was not a Kurdish option. The arrival of Ayatullah Khalkhali's revolutionary court, and its summary execution of at least 70 people, was likewise a sharp reminder of the consequences of capture. Kurdish troops withdrew to the hills, and on 4 and 5 September Iranian troops reoccupied Mahabad and Sardasht.

From that time the Kurdish forces lost all the towns to the government, but retained at least freedom of movement in the countryside. Ghassemlou himself insisted that war for five or more years was feasible, given the quantity of weapons captured from barracks the previous spring, and supplies smuggled in from Iraq and Turkey.

In Tehran growing concern at the failure to defeat the Kurds decisively, and the creeping loss of countryside to Kurdish guerrilla groups, prompted another attempt at negotiated settlement. In early November a government delegation visited Mahabad where it was greeted by crowds of several thousand, many of them armed and chanting their support for the KDPI. It promised to send Ghassemlou and Shaikh Izzedin a new offer from the government on the basis of their discussion.

In mid-December 1979 the government delivered its response, setting out the rights offered to minorities in a 14-Point document. It offered considerable freedom to locally constituted Provincial Councils, but in the view of Ghassemlou fell short of Kurdish requirements since it offered self-administration, not autonomy, and granted rights to the Kurds only as a religious (Sunni) minority, by implication denying the legitimacy of Kurdish identity. Furthermore there was considerable unhappiness over governmental insistence on the naming of police commanders for Kurdistan.

Disagreement over the limits to the area of 'self-administration' also thwarted agreement. The Kurds demanded western Azerbaijan, claiming its population as mainly Kurdish, whilst the government disagreed, claiming the majority were Azeri Turk. Likewise, the government refused to concede Ilam and Kermanshah on the grounds that the Kurds there were predominantly Shi'i, and this religious identity must take primacy over ethnicity. Failure to reach agreement gave way to fighting once more.

In mid-February 1980 Ghassemlou sought agreement with the newly elected President Bani Sadr, presenting a new plan which defined the Kurdish autonomous area by popular majority vote in the relevant areas, and ceded to central government responsibility for long-term economic planning, national defence and foreign policy. The plan was rejected out of hand, Bani Sadr insisting there could be no settlement until the Kurds laid down their arms, and Ghassemlou refusing this until the Kurdish question was satisfactorily settled.

Once more both sides resumed fighting, with the government reasserting control over the towns of Kurdistan, and the Kurds holding most of, if not all, the countryside. An area of roughly 120,000 sq. kms remained in Kurdish hands, but without a town of any size. Indefinite guerrilla war was in prospect, with neither side able to achieve its objective. In September 1980, however, Iraq repudiated the Algiers

Agreement and invaded Iran. For the Kurds of both Iran and Iraq, it offered the first opportunity since the birth of Kurdish nationalism to assert their aspirations in tandem.

The Iran-Iraq war and after

In retrospect, it is difficult to recognize just how great the opportunity for the Kurds appeared to be when Saddam Hussein decided to attack Iran. Already severely weakened by the Revolution, the government in Tehran seemed unlikely to be able to both absorb the shock waves of Iraq's attack and at the same time to recapture its Kurdish region. Saddam himself had counted on the disarray within the Iranian army to secure a rapid and conclusive victory which would return the Shatt al Arab to sole Iraqi control – thus erasing the humiliation of the Algiers Agreement – and possibly to establish Iraqi control over Khuzistan, the Arab province beyond the Shatt al Arab.

However, Iran rallied to the crisis. Its forces defended border towns a good deal more tenaciously than Baghdad had bargained for. By early 1982 Iran had recovered from the initial shock and had ejected the Iraqis from its territory. Furthermore, Tehran was able to make use of the KDP against the KDPI in the border area. There was little love lost between the two parties, since the KDP blamed the KDPI for the desecration of Mulla Mustafa Barzani's grave at Ushnavia. In mid-1982 Tehran was able to send its armed forces against the KDPI, and in November these forces recaptured the Piranshahr-Sardasht road, a serious loss to the KDPI on account of its value for the movement of troops and supplies to sustain a guerrilla war. In 1983 the Iranian army continued its ground offensive, establishing control of the high ground around Sardasht. By early 1984 the Kurdish-controlled region of Iran had been virtually eliminated. At least 27,500 Kurds were reckoned to have died by this stage, of whom only 2500 were fighters.

The loss of a territorial base in Iran, except for Hawraman, drove the KDPI and Komala to abandon the conventional guerrilla struggle they had waged until that time. Through the widespread network of sympathy throughout Iranian Kurdistan, both parties were able to reintegrate their pesh mergas into civilian areas. Each area was able to call on a number of fighters if need be for specific operations. In fact both parties 'stood down' most of their fighters, and used small groups for specific resistance operations. For the rest of the decade, Kurdish guerrilla operations took place largely after nightfall. Most attacks were upon army checkpoints on the roads of Kurdistan. Iraq continued to provide modest help to both KDPI and Komala until the ceasefire in August 1988.

Government treatment of its Kurdish opponents, as with its other opponents, at times seemed arbitrary and capricious. Almost certainly this reflected the power struggles taking place within the Iranian leadership. At the end of 1988 many of those Kurds already imprisoned perished in waves of mass killings which took place at the end of the year. The prime victims were members of Komala, for which the state had particular repugnance, deeming its Marxism to be atheistic. Official attitudes towards the KDPI seem to have been more tolerant, presumably in response to Ghassemlou's search for an accommodation with Tehran in 1988.

Ghassemlou's desire to reach a settlement reflected his own pessimism concerning the future of the armed struggle. Although guerrilla operations continued to be sustained in rural areas, there seemed little hope of this achieving much against the 200,000 government troops stationed in Iranian Kurdistan. Not everyone in KDPI accepted Ghassemlou's accommodation policy, and the party suffered a split in June 1988. Those who denounced Ghassemlou's policy, however, were almost entirely expatriates living in Paris who rapidly lost influence.

Despite the split in the KDPI, Ghassemlou pressed on with seeking an accommodation with Tehran. By 1988, the political manoeuvring in anticipation of the post-Khomeini era provided the opportunity for dialogue. Meetings took place at the end of 1988. But Ghassemlou was assassinated when he attended a secret meeting with Iranian representatives in Vienna in July 1989. The assassination was a serious blow for the Iranian Kurdish movement. Ghassemlou has proved impossible to replace. For many years he had been recognized as the most able politician of the whole Kurdish people. Furthermore, since there was little doubt that he had been killed by the very Iranian delegates with whom he had been negotiating, it put the whole feasibility of negotiation in doubt.

Komala, which seemed more important in the early 1980s, has declined and, compared with KDPI, has a significant following only around Sanandaj. This decline followed its unification with a small communist group to make a new 'Communist Party of Iran', in which Komala represents the local Kurdish section of the party. Komala, too, has been the target of assassination. One month after Ghassemlou's death, one of Komala's leaders was killed in Larnaca.[75]

Komala's relations with KDPI had deteriorated badly during the early phase of the Iran-Iraq war, and in November 1984 a KDPI commander was killed by Komala, sparking off a damaging series of armed clashes between the two parties. Relations remained very poor into the early 1990s.

Although the KDPI enjoys widespread popularity throughout Iranian Kurdistan, there is no question of it succeeding in the military struggle. Its nocturnal guerrilla activities, which make some roads risky after dark, remain easily containable by the security forces. The KDPI leadership recognizes that in spite of Ghassemlou's assassination, negotiations are the only route through which a measure of autonomy might be achieved. There is also a realization that as the religious and nationalist fervour of the Islamic Republic begins to abate, a cautiously liberalizing regime in Tehran might offer its Kurds a greater say in their community affairs. In the meantime Kurdistan, unlike the rest of Iran, remains effectively under military rather than civil government.

Human rights continue to be infringed. In spring 1991 there were rumours that Kurds who had been imprisoned for some time were summarily executed, as a warning to the populace against following the rebelliousness of Iraq's Kurds. In cultural matters there has been some relaxation. Permission to publish and sell materials in Kurdish – even if these are censored – marks a substantial departure from the regime under the Shahs. Some materials in Kurdish on Iranian or Kurdish political history have been marketed without difficulty. But discrimination on religious grounds persists. Shi'is are preferred for government appointments, just as Sunnis tend to be preferred in Turkey and Iraq.

10

THE KURDS IN IRAQ
– FROM THE MANDATE TO THE BA'TH

As a state, Iraq has recognized Kurdish rights to a greater say in internal affairs than either Iran or Turkey has done. Nevertheless it has also found itself involved in more major confrontations with the Kurds in recent years and is consequently more widely known as oppressive to the Kurds. However, as elsewhere, there has been a second important dimension to the Kurdish question, that of the internal conflicts within Kurdish society and the way these have interacted with the conflict with government to the detriment of Kurdish national aspirations.

The Kurds under the British mandate 1918-1932[76]

Modern Iraq emerged from the Ottoman provinces of Mesopotamia as a result of conquest by the British army in 1914-18. The conquest had not been easy, and it was 1917 before Baghdad fell. In May 1918 Kirkuk was captured, and Mosul was taken, despite Ottoman protests, a few days after the armistice of Mudros (30 October 1918). In a few weeks the Ottomans had withdrawn from all of Mosul province, as far north as Zakhu. At first the British had in mind the creation of an Arab state, and one or more semi-autonomous Kurdish provinces to be loosely attached to the Arab state, along the lines of President Wilson's Fourteen Points, and with the advantage to Britain of considerable control over the economic unity of the whole of Iraq, and particularly over oil reserves which fell within Mosul province.

There were good grounds for the establishment of a Kurdish province. The newly formed League of Nations Commission shortly after considered that:

'if the ethnic argument alone had to be taken into account, the necessary conclusion would be that an independent Kurdish State should be created, since the Kurds form five-eighths of the population.'[77]

Furthermore, of all the Muslim races (Arab, Turk and Kurd), the League of Nations Commission considered the Kurds lived on the most friendly terms with the considerable Christian minority (both Nestorians and Chaldeans). But the Kurds of Mosul vilayet were profoundly disunited amongst themselves:

> '*Of the Kurds who inhabit the disputed territory, those who live north of the Greater Zab are, as regards language, ethnic affinities, and personal and economic relations, more closely connected with the Kurds of... Turkey, whilst those who live south of the Lesser Zab have more in common with the Kurds of Persia*'.[78]

Even within these two zones the nomad tribes lived one life, the Kurdish sedentary tribesmen, peasants and townspeople another. Even the sedentary elements were divided, some into clans which, except under compulsion, were not accustomed to acknowledge any higher authority than their local chieftain. Kurdish national feeling was only expressed in a negative form: opposition to political control by outsiders.

Nothing, perhaps, expressed Kurdish disarray more than the effort of the British to establish whether their proposal that their protégé, the Emir Faisal, should become King of all Iraq was acceptable to the Kurdish population. Mosul and Arbil voted in favour, Kirkuk voted for a delay on its decision (decided in 1923 in favour of Faisal's Iraq), though the interesting fact is that its Kurds asked for a separate Kurdish province *but only on condition* that they were not incorporated with the Kurds of Sulaymaniya. Only the population of the latter voted unconditionally against Faisal or any inclusion in Iraq.

In order to administer whilst a political solution was evolved, Britain chose to work through the traditional Kurdish leadership. It was not successful. In Sulaymaniya, Britain invited Shaikh Mahmud Barzinji to act as governor in 1919, since he had done so for the Turks, on condition that he accepted British advice and orders. Shaikh Mahmud was extremely powerful locally, since he was both agha and shaikh. He was given an enlarged area, beyond his previous area of authority, which brought him into conflict with chiefs of other clans, particularly those of Kirkuk and Kufri, Zakho and Amadiya, and those of Barzan and Arbil. Even in Halabja and Panjwin, 20 miles from his capital of Sulaymaniya, he was unable to exert his authority unchallenged. And in Baghdad were Kurdish notable families long since absorbed into the establishment, for example the Babans, who were hostile to his ambition. So when Shaikh Mahmud challenged British authority in 1919, he was removed and exiled to India.

Early British administration of Kurdistan was also interrupted by the attempt of Kemalist Turks to re-establish Turkish control over the mountains as far south as Rowanduz in 1922. With much of Iraqi Kurdistan in ferment and liable to fall into pro-Turkish hands, the British recalled Shaikh Mahmud Barzinji, instructing him to adhere to British policy. However, Shaikh Mahmud entered into immediate correspondence with the Turks and thence into rebellion, crushed only when the British bombed his residence.

With the re-establishment of British control of Sulaymaniya, it was decided to incorporate the district into Iraq, with the agreement of a provisional Kurdish administration in Sulaymaniya whose only stipulation was that they would not continue in office if Shaikh Mahmud returned. When Britain withdrew its troops, this administration immediately resigned, fearing the wrath of the Shaikh and his supporters. When in summer 1923 Shaikh Barzinji proceeded to attack his neighbours, the British reprisals drove him out of Sulaymaniya.

Britain decided upon direct administration, through Kurdish officials, recognizing Kurdish culture, language and customs, but acting as supervisor which no other power, Iraqi or Kurd, at that time was in a position to do. During the negotiations with the Kemalists in Lausanne, a few Kurdish leaders petitioned Britain for a separate Kurdish state in Iraqi Kurdistan.[79] Rival Kurdish leaders – friendlier to Baghdad – pledged their loyalty to the Iraq government.

Neither the British, nor the League of Nations responsible for awarding Britain the mandate for Iraq, doubted that particularly in Sulaymaniya, if not elsewhere in Kurdistan, a Kurdish national feeling already existed, albeit still in rudimentary form. Nevertheless, the Kurds of Kirkuk would not be ruled by Sulaymaniya Kurds, least of all by Shaikh Mahmud, whilst within Sulaymaniya itself was a constituency of more educated Kurds opposed to him also. Furthermore the whole Kurdish area of Iraq was tied economically to the market towns and cities on the plain, which were predominantly Arab or Turkoman.

Britain hoped therefore that the Kurds would be reconciled to incorporation within Arab Iraq. The Iraq Government had pledged itself to honour the League of Nations' recommendations that the Kurds be allowed to use their language, both in schools and in local administration (not easy since there were a number of dialects, but certainly possible to standardize), and that Kurds should comprise the administration of the region. But these pledges were not included in the Anglo-Iraqi treaty of 1930 which accorded Iraq its independence (implemented 1932). The Kurds naturally felt unsafe without written guarantees. Moreover, no steps had been taken on the sensitive language issue, either to standardize the language or to train teachers or to produce textbooks. In 1926 shortly before his resignation the Iraqi Prime Minister, Abd al Muhsin al Sa'dun, had declared:

> *'This nation cannot live unless it gives all Iraqi elements their rights...*
> *The fate of Turkey should be a lesson to us and we should not revert to*
> *the policy formerly pursued by the Ottoman Government. We should*
> *give the Kurds their rights. Their officials should be from among them:*
> *their tongue should be their official language and their children should*
> *learn their own tongue in the schools. It is incumbent upon us to treat*
> *all elements, whether Muslim or non-Muslim, with fairness and justice,*
> *and give them their rights.'[80]*

His advice went unheeded. This was partly out of governmental inertia, but also partly out of apprehension that whatever special privileges were granted to the Kurds, the Shi'ia community of southern Iraq might demand similar ones.

The role of Mulla Mustafa Barzani

No sooner was the handover of Mosul to Iraq under way than Shaikh Mahmud Barzinji revolted, calling for a united Kurdistan. In spring 1931 he was defeated, and accepted town arrest for himself and his family in southern Iraq. Other Kurds demanded more moderate safeguards, but the government was unwilling to consider them. British officials remained embarrassed and dissatisfied with the government's pusillanimous steps to accommodate Kurdish feeling. Strikes and demonstrations in Sulaymaniya followed, perhaps the first real evidence of popular Kurdish aspirations in Iraq, since these were carried out by workers, merchants and townspeople.

With the arrest of Shaikh Mahmud Barzinji, another Kurdish chief took up a position of leadership amongst Kurdish 'separatists'. That man was Mulla Mustafa Barzani, destined to become almost synonymous with Kurdish revolt until his death in 1979.[81] Barzani was important, not only for his prolonged resistance to Baghdad, but also because he was a classic representative of the shaikhly establishment, combining the secular power of an agha with that of religious (and charismatic) leadership.

Barzan was a remote village in north-eastern Iraq, since time immemorial an area of lawlessness and tribal warfare, barely touched by any government ever. Mulla Mustafa's grandfather, Muhammad, had been prominent in the Naqshbandi order, and was the first Barzani to bring the family to prominence. As a result of the following he created, both he and his descendants became temporal and spiritual leaders of the area. As he was to prove, even 40 years on, no other Kurd could so rally rank and file Kurds, to the chagrin of those Kurds who wished to do away with the old order along with Turkish and Iraqi rule.

Mulla Mustafa's first clash with the authorities was in connection with government attempts to settle Assyrian Christian refugees from Hakkari[82] on land adjacent to Barzan, and with attempts to introduce police and taxation into the area. He, his elder brother Ahmad, and their family surrendered to the Turks over the border, but were amnestied in 1933. Ten years later he escaped to Barzan and resumed his conflict with the government, assisted by Kurdish nationalists, an indication that the Barzani family had acquired a more nationalist hue. By 1945 he was effective ruler in a wide area, intervening in inter-tribal disputes, and in the government distribution of supplies, and repelling attempts by the Iraqi army to defeat him. However, in late 1945 he was pushed over the border into Iran, where he threw in his lot with the Kurdish Democratic Party (KDP) in Mahabad. He spent the next 12 years in exile in the USSR.

There is a sense in which the conduct of neither the government nor the Kurdish people was likely to satisfy the other. Government decisions to introduce education and other benefits were lackadaisical in implementation, but had they been more rigorously pursued these would undoubtedly have eventually caused conflict within Kurdish society. As it was, the rule that officials in Kurdish areas must be Kurds or Kurdish-speaking began to undermine the position of both shaikh and agha, and to strengthen that of government since the agha was no longer the only intermediary with the civil service.

Mulla Mustafa was able to return to Iraq following the coup of 1958 carried out by General Qasim against the Hashemite monarchy.[83] Barzani's relationship with Qasim and with neighbouring Kurds reflected the need of any aspiring chief to recognition from government and neighbours in order to fulfil his objectives. From the moment of his return, Barzani established a close and friendly relationship with Qasim. On the other hand, he immediately took a vigorous part in the still not legalized KDP, using the prestige that rested on his own tribal following and allies (at least 6000 fighting men) who out-numbered any other Kurdish force, to persuade the KDP Politburo to accept his protégé, and erstwhile Party Secretary, Hamza Abdullah, back into the Party and subsequently back into his old post. When he found himself opposed by Abdullah, however, his men stormed KDP headquarters and evicted him.

Barzani willingly co-operated with Qasim in the defeat of the latter's Arab nationalist and pro-monarchist enemies. In March 1959 Barzani's Kurds assisted in the massacre following an abortive rising in Mosul. Then he co-operated with the Communists to attack mutual Turkoman enemies in Kirkuk, another act that suited Qasim. Shortly after, however, he turned on his erstwhile Communist allies at Qasim's bidding. Barzani was rewarded with the legalization of the KDP, thus strengthening his hand further in the party, with the restoration of Barzani land confiscated by the Hashemites, and with support against 'anti-government' Kurds.

These 'anti-government' Kurds were long-standing enemies of the Barzani family, as well as supporters of the previous regime. Some of them, the neighbouring Zibaris for example, had been in feud with the Barzanis since the beginning of the century or earlier. Others, the Baradost, Herki and Surchi tribes, had been given confiscated Barzan land in return for helping the Hashemites defeat Barzani in the 1930s and 1940s. Thus the conflict reflected deepseated internal Kurdish feuds, and different Kurd – government alliances, as well as any nationalist ingredient.

When Barzani managed to assassinate the Zibari chief in 1960, Qasim began to realize that he had been greatly mistaken in not restraining Barzani and not cultivating a counterbalance within Kurdistan. Qasim started to discourage Barzani from his implacable pursuit of old enemies, and began quietly to encourage and then arm some of Barzani's adversaries. By the end of 1960 his break with Barzani was an open secret.

In 1961 Barzani tried to fulfil Kurdish expectations from the new Constitution by demanding a substantial degree of autonomy for the Kurdish region. But by then he probably realized that Qasim was unlikely to co-operate further with him, not least because to accede to Barzani's demands would raise the prestige and power of the latter in Kurdish circles still further, particularly in the KDP. Qasim had already gone further than the preceding regime in recognizing Kurdish rights. Kurdish activities had dramatically increased. The new constitution had accorded the Kurds an unprecedented position:

'The Kurds and Arabs are partners within this nation. The Constitution guarantees their rights within the framework of the Iraqi Republic.'[84]

Several Kurds had been appointed to senior office. Kurdish publications flourished.

Although he had plenty of enemies in Kurdistan, Barzani knew he could count on a number of disaffected aghas. Some of these regretted the passing of the Hashemites. They had a practical reason for doing so, because Qasim's much publicized agrarian reform law struck at the landlord class. Furthermore Barzani and these aghas could rely on the tribesmen following their lead partly on account of unpopular new land and tobacco taxes. He therefore was content to allow his fight with the Baghdad-supported Zibaris in winter 1960-61 to drift into widespread revolt against Qasim.

The KDP at first did not join the revolt, and only did so with reluctance when its hand was forced by Qasim's proscription of the party. The KDP membership, and particularly the Politburo, had been uneasy by the way in which Barzani had so easily been able to assume personal leadership on his return from exile. Barzani had played an important part in the KDP since 1946 but the conflict between his own traditional view and that of urban and leftist elements had never been resolved. In 1946 Barzani had worsted the leftists, but in 1953 during his exile these – amongst whom Ibrahim Ahmad and Jalal Talabani of the Politburo were pre-eminent – asserted their collective leadership. Their unease at Barzani's personality cult, strength and autocratic behaviour was shared by others.

It was a clash between party democracy and traditional tribal leadership, and the old conflict traceable to the earlier years of nationalism in Kurdistan found new expression in the quarrels within the KDP. This unsatisfactory and largely unresolved situation resulted in the lack of a clear national goal, the predominance of tribal elements and loyalties that frequently frustrated nationalist activities. Kurdish revolts 'were motivated as much by concepts of honour and pride, possibilities of financial gain, and a desire to struggle against the encroaching authority of the government as by nationalist goals'.[85]

Iraq's neighbours used the war to their own advantage. Turkey, hostile to Qasim, was happy to adopt a benevolent neutralism, allowing Iraqi Kurds to move through Turkish territory in their war with Baghdad so long as they did not export their separatism to their own Kurds. Iran was more positive in its support for Kurdish rebels though, like Turkey's, conditional on Iraqi Kurdish understanding that Kurdish separatism was not for export to Iran. Barzani was willing to go along with these stipulations.

Baghdad's war against the Kurds became one of the more constant realities of life in Iraq. Qasim was overthrown in February 1963 by

Ba'this, who themselves were ousted later on in the year by Abd el Salam Arif. He quickly negotiated a ceasefire with Barzani in February 1964.

The acceptance of a ceasefire led to a sharp split between Barzani and the KDP Politburo, led by Ibrahim Ahmad and Jalal Talabani. This was formally on the grounds that the party had not been consulted, and also because Barzani had settled with a government offering less than Qasim had done in 1958, accepting the disbandment of the Kurdish forces. Behind these open criticisms was a more fundamental one to do with Barzani's methods of operation and objectives. His style was wholly alien to the nationalism of the urban intelligentsia which called for consultation and consensus. Barzani's response was to chase the Politburo into Iran by force of arms. He had no difficulty doing so, since he controlled most of Iraqi Kurdistan, and had larger and more dependable forces.

Given its urban leadership, it is not surprising that the Politburo held sway only in the lower hills and towns. Its 'programme of political education, establishing village councils, combating illiteracy and collecting taxes frightened and angered feudal leaders, who already saw the KDP as an enemy'.[86] There was another important factor. Most of the Politburo leadership came from the Sulaymaniya region, whilst Barzani's stronghold lay in the north. The two areas belonged to different dialect regions, Sorani and Kurmanji respectively. Despite temporary reconciliations, Barzani and the KDP Politburo continued to feud, with the latter rejecting his leadership in 1967.

The ceasefire did not hold. However, in order to undercut Talabani of the Politburo, who was also trying to negotiate with the government, Barzani agreed to a truce in 1966. Shortly after, he agreed to a Baghdad twelve-point programme (July 1966) which went a considerable way towards meeting Kurdish demands. But the government of Premier Bazzaz fell before it could implement the programme, and an uneasy relationship continued, with armed clashes, until the Ba'th coup of 1968.

11

THE KURDS IN IRAQ
– UNDER THE BA'TH

The Ba'th and Barzani had already had a taste of each other during the shortlived Ba'th government of 1963. Immediately after the coup in February 1963, both sides had willingly accepted a ceasefire and begun the search for agreement. However, after a preliminary agreement both sides began to back away. Each side agreed to things one day, but rejected them the next. The Ba'th distrusted Barzani because their party members had been amongst those killed when Barzani had helped to destroy Qasim's enemies in 1959. Barzani was also upset by Ba'th negotiations with the United Arab Republic with a view to joining Syria and Egypt in union, a feeling only intensified when his enemy Talabani went to Cairo with Ba'th approval to obtain assurances from Nasser of the latter's support for a fair deal for the Kurds.

In June 1963 the fight between Barzani and Baghdad had commenced when his negotiating team was arrested and the Iraqi army started a brutal onslaught against Barzani's forces. Barzani and the KDP responded, attacking army posts, ambushing army vehicles and burning anti-Barzani Kurdish villages, but soon lost territory to the Iraq army which was considerably assisted by tribes hostile to Barzani. But the army was baulked by the onset of winter, strife within the Ba'th regime, and the skill of the Kurds in mountain warfare. With the overthrow of the Ba'th in November 1963, Baghdad's effort to defeat the Kurds collapsed.

The Ba'th regime had actually offered the Kurds more than any previous Iraqi government (or any Turkish or Iranian government for that matter) had done.[87] When the Ba'th resumed power by coup in 1968 the resolution of the Kurdish question in a peaceful manner was once again a major feature of its programme, and it proposed a resumption of the 1966 peace plan proposed by the previous government of Prime Minister Bazzaz. However, it again ran into trouble with Barzani. Both sides viewed each other with enormous suspicion, and the Ba'this felt bitter that Barzani had been willing to accept lesser offers from successor governments after the anti-Ba'th coup of 1963 in which Barzani had co-operated. For his part, Barzani could not forget that the Ba'th had led the toughest assault ever on Kurdistan and had solicited the assistance of hostile Kurdish tribes.

There was another reason for Ba'th-Barzani wariness. The Ba'th and the Talabani faction of the KDP were natural allies ideologically, since both were leftist and both advocated (in principle at any rate) Kurd—Arab fraternity. Barzani might easily be left out in the cold, and he could not afford that, particularly since he remained at enmity with Talabani. When the proposed peaceful solution for the Kurdish question was announced, based on equality of national rights and duties, Talabani's KDP welcomed it. Barzani's faction of KDP treated it with caution and scepticism.

Undoubtedly Talabani hoped that the government would view his wing of the KDP as the natural ally of the Ba'th, and thus the official representative of the Kurds. Within Kurdistan, his clashes with Barzani's KDP were supported by the army. It seemed as if Talabani could win. Although numerically smaller, he held most of the Kurdish towns in the mountains, and enjoyed the backing of a professional army. But in reality he was competing not only with a numerically stronger force, but one based on tribal loyalty, loyalty to the charisma of the Kurds' historic leader, and one that drew its rank and file from the remotest villages. These were the toughest and most skilled at mountain warfare. Furthermore Barzani enjoyed considerable material support from outside. The Shah, who had little love for the Ba'th regime, was one source of support, and the CIA and Israel were others.

Two other factors helped to defeat Talabani. Many Kurds, having successfully fought throughout the 1960s, genuinely believed they could defeat the Iraqi army and establish an independent state. By apparently siding with Baghdad Talabani compromised his position in the eyes of many Kurds. In a world of absolute loyalties, Talabani was easily viewed as a traitor, and it was not difficult for Barzani to portray him as such. Talabani's lack of success against Barzani on the battlefield persuaded the Ba'th, or at any rate Saddam Hussein who at this time was trying to assert himself within the Ba'th, that he must be abandoned and Barzani negotiated with, if the question was to be settled peacefully.

The peace agreement of 1970

The new efforts at dialogue commenced with Barzani from late 1969 brought about a ceasefire and the declaration of a peace agreement on 11 March 1970. Disagreements during this period centred not on the question of Kurdish national rights, but on Barzani's insistence that the government end its relations with the Talabani-Ahmad faction of KDP, and disband its Kurdish irregulars composed of anti-Barzani tribal elements. The government had to abandon its wish to act as moderator between the two factions, and complied with Barzani's demand.

In human terms the cost of a decade of conflict had been high. According to a United Nations mission, 40,000 houses had been destroyed in 700 villages. 300,000 people had been displaced or made homeless. Others estimated 60,000 casualties, killed and wounded. It said that there were several civilian massacres, probably carried out mostly by the Iraqi army, though the killing of civilians by Barzani's men cannot be ruled out.

The Agreement recognized the bi-national character of the Iraqi state, in which the Kurds were to be free and equal partners, and included the following:

1. Participation of the Kurds in government, including the appointment of Kurds to key posts in the state;
2. Recognition of Kurdish in those areas where Kurds constitute the majority. Kurdish and Arabic would be taught together in all schools;
3. Furtherance of Kurdish education and culture;
4. Requirement that officials in the Kurdish areas speak Kurdish;
5. Right to establish Kurdish student, youth, womens' and teachers' organizations;
6. Economic development of the Kurdish area;
7. Return of Kurds to their villages or financial compensation;
8. Agrarian reform;
9. Amendment of the constitution to read: '*the Iraqi people consist of two main nationalities: the Arab and Kurdish nationalities*';
10. Return of the clandestine radio and heavy weapons to the government;
11. Appointment of a Kurdish vice-president;
12. Amendment of provincial laws in accordance with this declaration;
13. Formation of a Kurdish area with self-government.

The Agreement committed the government to implementation within four years.[88]

Afterwards Barzani declared:

> 'At first they [the Ba'thists] came to us and said, "We will grant you self-rule." I said this was a ruse. I knew it even before I signed the agreement. But [our] people asked me, "How can you refuse self-rule for the Kurdish people?"'[89]

Why then did Barzani go along with Baghdad? One must conclude that in addition to Kurdish war-weariness and the knowledge that Iranian support was limited to discomfiture of Baghdad rather than to Kurdish victory, Barzani saw the opportunity to consolidate his own position within the Kurdish movement to the detriment of the Talabani-Ahmad faction. If the government reneged, he could always take to the hills once more, as undisputed Kurdish leader.

During 1970 a number of clauses of the agreement were implemented, including the amendment to the constitution (9 above), the appointment of senior Kurdish officials including senior members of the KDP as governors of Dohuk and Arbil respectively, Kurdish police chiefs for the three Kurdish provinces of Dohuk, Arbil and Sulaymaniya (1). Factories were established (6), and agrarian reform quickened (8).

Apparently, secret agreements were also implemented. Talabani found himself isolated whilst Ibrahim Ahmad went to London for prolonged medical treatment, and their newspaper was shut down. Kurdish irregular troops, tribal enemies of Barzani, were disbanded. Despite criticisms of government sluggishness, Kurdish figures speak for themselves. Within a year of the agreement, construction had begun on hospitals and schools, and over 2700 houses had been built or rebuilt in the area. Everything seemed bound for success.

Why, then, did the agreement fall apart? Certainly each side doubted the sincerity of the other. In summer 1972 Barzani, encouraged by Iran, the United States and Israel, consolidated his control of the Kurdish area, and increased his demands to include wider military and political authority, making provocative statements about foreign support. The difficulties with Baghdad centred on particular issues, such as the delineation of the Kurdish area, the manner of KDP participation in government, and continued Kurdish relations with Iran. It was on account of the latter that the Ba'th refused the candidature of the KDP's secretary as Vice-President (11). The Kurds were unable to agree on an alternative, and they recognized – as did everyone else – that the post was symbolic, devoid of political power.

The census to establish where Kurds formed a majority was another bone of contention. It was repeatedly postponed, at first by mutual agreement. The Ba'th did not wish to cede Kirkuk to the Kurdish area on account of its oil, and was probably reluctant to ascertain which community was the majority amongst the Arabs, Kurds and substantial Turkoman population. The latter was no longer as hostile as it had been to the Kurds, and some viewed Kurdish rule as preferable to that of the Ba'th. Barzani accused the government of introducing Arabs into Kirkuk and other areas to change the demographic balance, and the government responded by offering to use the 1965 or 1957 census instead. The dispute also centred on the expulsion of the Failli Kurds, who were considered by the Ba'th to be Iranian, but who were living in Iraq though without Iraqi citizenship. The government was fearful that Turkish or Iranian Kurds were being introduced into the area to tip the scales in critical areas like Kirkuk.

Clashes occurred between government and Barzani forces. The Kurds accused the government of increasing its forces in the Kurdish area, whilst the government, rather than denying it, justified their presence on the grounds of Iranian threats along the border. The government believed that the border guards, who were under Barzani's control and until the ceasefire had been *pesh mergas* (Kurdish freedom fighters – literally, 'those who face death'), were abetting Iranian infringements of the border. It may well have suspected Barzani of encouraging Iran to put pressure on Baghdad.

On 29 September 1971 the situation deteriorated greatly with an unsuccessful attempt on Barzani's life. The government was the obvious and prime suspect. There was a second attempt in 1972, and by September the Ba'th called for 'forestalling any further deteriorating relations between the two parties',[90] listing those clauses already implemented and those not already in force. It also claimed evidence of Kurdish-Iranian ties, including the continued flow of arms across the border and other evidence, and also the serious charge of large-scale acts of rape committed by pesh mergas, and the burning of villages known to be loyal to the government. Whether or not these were true, the government demanded that the border be sealed forthwith and that the KDP ensure discipline and lawful behaviour amongst its supporters. The KDP replied with similar accusations against the government, the most serious of which remained the question of Arabization of Kirkuk and environs. For an outsider it was virtually impossible to tell which side was being less truthful. There seemed to be considerable bad faith on both sides. The dispute became increasingly public. Efforts by the Soviets to mediate were unsuccessful.

It was the involvement of other foreign powers in Iraq—Kurdish affairs that gave the Ba'th cause for even greater concern that Barzani was acting against the state from the earliest days of the Agreement. These acts included: the establishment of a sophisticated intelligence apparatus with the help of Iranian SAVAK and Israeli Mossad in order to gather intelligence on Iraq and its armed forces; a public promise to turn Kirkuk oilfield over to American companies in return for US aid; appeals for US aid as early as 1971. Two weeks after the nationalization of the Iraq Petroleum Company in 1972, the US government responded to Barzani. The US wanted to neutralize the danger of Iraqi damage to its interests in the region, particularly in relation to Iran and Israel. In 1972 the fact of Israeli support of $US 50,000 monthly (so it was rumoured) for Barzani became public knowledge with a report by the American columnist, Jack Anderson, based on a CIA report. In fact, Israeli provision of arms and advisers dates back to the early 1960s.

For the Kurds the tragedy of such support was that it was provided to encourage Barzani to wage war on Baghdad but not to achieve autonomy. If the Kurds won outright they would cease to be the debilitating factor against the Ba'th that the US, Iran and Israel all wanted. It was vital therefore to ensure both that the Kurds continued to fight Baghdad, but also that they would never win.

Barzani's dealings with those foreign powers most hostile to Iraq created the greatest possible anxiety in Baghdad. The Ba'th was fearful of full-scale war with the Kurds again. The civil wing feared it would give an opportunity to the military wing of the party to take over power, and both wings feared that it might trigger an anti-Ba'th coup, as had occurred in 1963.

At the beginning of 1974 the crisis came to a head over the effect of nationalization of Kirkuk oil production. Barzani and the KDP insisted on a 'proportional distribution of oil revenues', whilst the Ba'th insisted that these were national assets to be allocated under central authority. The Ba'th was very sensitive on the question since it could hardly give part or all of its oil to Barzani who had already expressed the intention of handing over exploitation to an American company. The Ba'th 'viewed the Kurdish claim as tantamount to the establishment of a confederation'.[91]

The other bone of contention centred on the degree of autonomy the KDP was demanding. The KDP was very suspicious that Ba'th arrangements would not yield true autonomy. The Ba'th viewed KDP demands as an attempt to create a state within a state, with its insistence on the establishment of the Kurdish administrative centre in Kirkuk (itself a disputed area), and 'mixed administration' where the population was mixed. The Ba'th was unwilling to concede, had lost patience (as no doubt the KDP had also), and invited KDP support of the Autonomy Law to be announced on 11 March 1974. The KDP was given 14 days in which to respond with assent, in order to participate in government.

The Ba'th may well have thought that the Kurds were divided and undecided how to proceed, and that it could therefore impose its own position. New splits had occurred within Kurdish ranks in early 1974. Two KDP Central Committee members broke with Barzani, accusing him of rejecting democratic practices, of kidnapping and executing a number of Kurdish leaders, and of identifying the destiny of the Kurds with himself (an understandable shortcoming for any charismatic leader). One of these, Hashim Aqrawi, took his followers into the Ba'th's Progressive National Front, on account of Barzani's accepting US and Israeli aid. Mulla Mustafa's own eldest son, Ubaidallah, also broke with his father since he:

> *'does not want self-rule to be implemented even if he was given Kirkuk and all its oil. His acceptance of the Law [Autonomy] will take everything from him, and he wants to remain absolute ruler'.*[92]

Had his son put his finger on Barzani's greatest flaw as Kurdish leader? There are reasons for thinking so. With the integration of Kurdistan into the Iraqi state on the basis of creating an autonomous administrative structure that would regularize and develop the region, there could be little place for a traditionalist tribal leader. Autonomy would mark the end of rule by chiefs. Did Barzani perceive this, and therefore, as his son asserted, ensure the Agreement could not succeed?

The Autonomy Declaration of 1974

The Autonomy Law was an emasculated version of the 1970 agreement, offering less than the KDP had demanded, but admittedly a great deal more than the Kurds in Iran or Turkey dared hope for. Its general provisions were:[93]

> *1. The area of Kurdistan shall enjoy autonomy, limited by the legal, political and economic integrity of the Republic of Iraq. The area shall be defined in accordance with the 11 March 1970 manifesto, and the 1957 census records.*
>
> *2. Kurdish will be the official language beside Arabic in the region, and the language of education, although the teaching of Arabic will also be compulsory.*

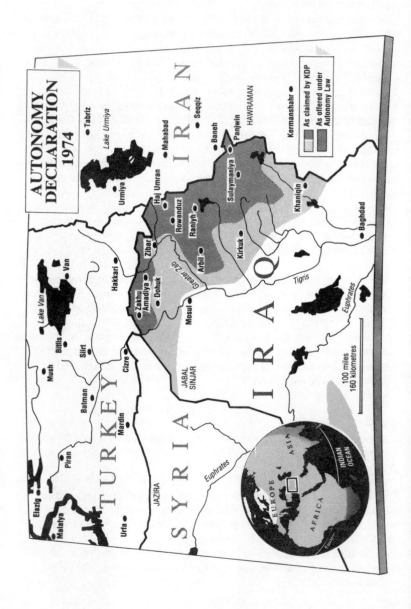

3. The rights of non-Kurdish minorities within the region will be guaranteed, with proportional representation in local autonomy.

4. The judiciary will conform with the legal system of Iraq.

5-9. These covered fiscal aspects of autonomy, within the financial integrity of the state.

10-15. These provided for the establishment of a Legislative and an Executive Council as governing organs of the autonomous area.

16-21. These established the relationship between the Central authority and the Autonomous Administration, defined by the government as one of supervision and co-ordination.

Whilst the Ba'th acknowledged through the Autonomy Law the existence of the Kurds as a distinct group in a region where they formed the majority of the population, and granted this group a level of autonomy, it also imposed such limits on this autonomy that effective authority remained in the hands of central government.

The Kurdish leadership rejected the Autonomy Law, mainly because of their unsatisfied demands for Kirkuk. But behind the diplomatic scenes Barzani had already asked for, and received, assurances from US officials in Iran. He is reported to have told these officials:

'This is what they have to use against us. If you will give us arms to match those arms, we will fight. Otherwise we will make peace. We don't want to be massacred.'[94]

Barzani confirmed the veracity of this deal subsequently:

'Were it not for American promises we would never have become trapped and involved to such an extent.'[95]

Hostilities began after the expiry of the 14-day period, developing into a full-scale war in April. Barzani was well placed. In addition to the extensive assurances of external aid, through Iran, he could also call on pesh merga, the Kurdish army, which was now 40,000 strong, with another 60,000 militiamen. From as far afield as Baghdad, he was joined by 60 doctors, 4500 teachers, 5000 policemen, 160 engineers and 100 army officers, evidence of the wide support Barzani enjoyed in the Kurdish population. By the end of April, however, the government had retaken Zakho and the Khabur Bridge on the Iraqi-Turkish border, demonstrating a vigour and ability that surprised many observers. Barzani sought heavy weapons from the US, but the latter declined the request. In mid-summer the Kurds were driven from most of the larger valleys, and by the onset of winter the strategic towns of Amadiya, Rowanduz, Raniya and Qala Diza had been lost to the government. The Kurds retreated higher into the mountains. By the end of the summer the Iraqi army controlled more areas of Kurdistan than at any time since 1961 and it was clear that the Kurds could only survive with major Iranian assistance.

Alarmed at Iraqi success, Iran increased support of the Kurds, providing long-range heavy artillery support (which the Iraqis could not match) and possibly Iranian troops dressed as Kurds. Iraq, because of its heavy losses, was bent upon defeating the Kurds before the onset of winter. Iran was likewise bent upon prolonging the struggle into the spring, since it knew how unpopular the war was in Iraq, and that it might unseat the Ba'th regime. There was speculation that the army might abandon the campaign against the Kurds and march south to seize Baghdad. However, unlike in previous campaigns, the Iraqi army held their positions in the mountains during the bitter winter months.

Fighting intensified in early 1975 when the government decided to push the 60,000 or so Kurdish troops from the strip they still controlled near the border with Iran. The Kurds were backed by Iranian heavy guns operating inside Iraqi territory and using missiles to bring down Iraqi fighters inside Iraqi territory. The Iraqis found that the Kurds with their Iranian artillery could not only hold their own but actually shell Arbil. The war reached a point where Iraq could not win unless Iranian support was cut off, and failing that faced the prospect of all-out war with Iran. Neither country wanted this.

Efforts by other Arab governments resulted in bringing the Shah and Iraqi Vice-President Saddam Hussein together in Algiers. On 15 March their agreement was made public. Iraq ceded its claim to the whole of the long-disputed Shatt al Arab waterway (the Tigris/Euphrates outlet south of Basra to the Gulf) and accepted the Thalweg Line partition (down the middle of the watercourse). Iran and Iraq affirmed:

'the re-establishment of mutual security and confidence along their joint borders and an undertaking to conduct strict and effective control along the joint borders to put a final end to all subversive infiltration from either side'.[96]

This was Iran's reciprocal gift, the sealing of its border to the Kurdish insurgents.

The Algiers agreement destroyed any Kurdish prospect of sustaining the war. On 23 March the KDP, following a visit by Barzani to the Shah, decided to give up the fight. Some rejected Barzani's leadership and decided to continue the struggle. Others accepted the amnesty before its expiry on 1 April. Barzani and several thousand pesh mergas withdrew into Iran, from where he himself went to the United States. Thousands of other Kurds decided to turn in their weapons and return home.

The human cost of the war had been enormous, at least 7000 dead and 10,000 wounded on the Iraqi side. The KDP admitted losing 2000 men but probably lost a good deal more. The grand total, for killed and wounded on both sides, probably totalled something in the order of 50,000. It also resulted in enormous civilian hardship. Up to 250,000 Kurds fled across the border to Iran. The total number of displaced persons was probably in the order of 600,000.

The majority of returnees from Iran were allowed to resume their normal life but many thousands, amongst whom were those who had deserted the Iraqi army in favour of Barzani, were resettled in the Arab provinces of Diwaniyya, Nasiriyya and Amara. In addition the Iraqis demolished up to 50 villages in the sensitive border areas with Iran and Turkey in order to create a 10-20km deep *cordon sanitaire*, moving the population down to the plain. Some Kurds were moved from peripheral Kurdish areas like Sinjar and Khanaqin. Late returnees, in October 1975, were automatically resettled outside the Kurdish area on the assumption that they must be hostile to have refused the earlier amnesty.

There is bitter disagreement over the numbers involved, but between 40,000 and 300,000 people were resettled. These draconian measures brought protests not only from Kurdish opponents of the regime but also from its supporters who, whilst approving the notion of a cordon sanitaire along the border, could not possibly give assent to the mass displacement of people from their homelands. Allegedly 1400 villages were affected by deportation, including another 300,000 Kurds moved out of the new border security zone and installed in 'strategic hamlets'. In 1976 these Kurdish critics persuaded Saddam Hussein to reverse the process, and by the end of that year the only large group remaining in southern Iraq, according to the government, were Barzani tribesmen and dependents, numbering some 6000 or so. Kurdish opposition continued to claim as many as 250,000 being kept in southern Iraq, and the government did admit to resettling Arabs in Khanaqin and Sulaymaniya, though it is difficult to establish whether the number involved was substantial.

Inside the Kurdish area the government took major steps to mollify the population. It claims that every family received 500 dinars, and further compensation was paid to every resettled family. It also claims building 32,000 new homes in model villages, though these were in the infamous 'strategic hamlets' in the security zone. Another 30,000 homes were built in Sulaymaniya, Duhok and Arbil. Inside the model villages the inhabitants are 'protected' by Iraqi troops, and are unable to find work. This has not only produced considerable social problems but also made it far easier for Iraq to recruit Kurds into the army, particularly after the war with Iran commenced. Altogether the government allocated 336,862 million dinars (about $US1.15 billion) to the rehabilitation programme at its outset, mainly to create some infrastructure. Land was reallocated to limit land ownership in the autonomous area, and almost 100,000 Kurdish peasant families benefited. Student enrolment jumped from 113,000 in 1974 to 333,000 in 1978.

Nevertheless, just as the army had acted with ruthlessness to crush the insurgents (with accusations of using poison gas against civilians), so also the government was charged with human rights violations by a number of organizations. In 1979 Amnesty International noted a report alleging the detention of 760 Kurds and the execution of another 200 Kurds since the collapse of the revolt.

In a memorandum to the United Nations, a new Kurdish opposition party, the PUK, accused Baghdad of the following violations of human rights: the execution of at least 150 Kurdish political prisoners; the forceful eviction of Kurds from many villages listed in the memorandum falling in the provinces of Kirkuk, Shaikhan, Zakho, Sinjar and Zimar; illegal seizure of land by the government; settlement of Arab tribes in Kurdish areas; the systematic retirement or transfer of Kurdish civil servants, police and soldiers.

The defeat of 1975 was the most serious one that the Iraqi Kurds had sustained. Barzani departed for the US where he died of cancer in March 1979. It is easy to be critical of Barzani, for his autocratic behaviour, for his public advocacy of US and Iranian assistance, and for his ruthless attitude towards his co-nationals in Iran. However, it is important to remember that it was his prowess on the battlefield which gave the Kurds something to be proud of. His feats were told and retold, acquiring mythical proportions, and they are likely to continue to be told for a long time to come. Barzani was a superhero, and given his style of shaikh and agha, he was a unique focus for emotional loyalty. Like Said Piran in Turkey in 1925, he appealed to national identity. Even though this may not be why men followed him, his appeal strengthened national consciousness amongst tribally minded people. By his feats he did far more to galvanize the Kurds than the political and intellectual propaganda plied by other nationalists, much of which must have left ordinary mountain villagers baffled. His charisma has effortlessly crossed the international borders of the region and was largely responsible for the rapid spread of national awareness amongst Turkish Kurds until the rise of the PKK.

Barzani left behind a vacuum that was hard to fill. The KDP broke into several factions, the leading one of which, the KDP Provisional Command, was led by his two loyal sons, Idris and Mas'ud. Only the 'official' KDP (a group led by Hashim Aqrawi, who had broken with Barzani in 1974) participated in the autonomy scheme in Iraqi Kurdistan. The real initiative was seized by a new party, the Patriotic Union of Kurdistan (PUK), formed by Jalal Talabani in June 1975. The PUK was the first to put 'partisans' into the field, backed by Syria (Iraq's ideological enemy). Talabani had two scores to settle, one with Barzani's KDP and the other with the government that had ditched him so suddenly in 1969. Talabani's strongholds were close to the Turkish border, and it was here that many fierce clashes took place both with Barzani and government forces from 1976 onwards.

When the Shah was overthrown in early 1979, different Kurdish groups sought Tehran's favour. Talabani's PUK and Mas'ud Barzani's KDP both publicly supported the revolution. Was Talabani, as Mulla Mustafa Barzani scathingly once remarked, 'an agent for everybody'?[97] Some Kurds thought so. In any case it was the KDP that made a successful alliance with the Islamic government in Tehran, by its support of the new Islamic government in its struggle against Kurdish autonomists in Iran. It was partly motivated by anger at the exhumation of the corpse of Mulla Mustafa from the grave at Ushnavia in Iranian Kurdistan, for which it held KDPI responsible. By embarking on a bitter struggle against the Iranian KDP, and its leftist allies, Mas'ud Barzani caused dismay amongst a Kurdish community more politically aware than it had been in his father's day.

Within the more traditionalist ranks of the Kurdish national struggle the conflict between 'tribal elements' and the intelligentsia had remained a major problem. This was manifest at the KDP's (it had dropped 'Provisional Command') ninth congress held in Iran in 1979. Idris Barzani was considered leader of the traditionalists, whilst his brother Mas'ud sought rapprochement with the intellectuals. Furthermore, the price of alliance with Iran, and the automatic 'succession' of the Barzani brothers to their father's political inheritance caused another major split, and the formation of a new splinter group, the Kurdistan Popular Democratic Party (KPDP) by Sami Abdul Rahman and Nur Shawis.

12

KURDS BETWEEN WARRING STATES – THE IRAN-IRAQ WAR

The Iran-Iraq War 1980-1985

The invasion of Iran by Iraq in September 1980, and the consequent bloody stalemate between the two giants, opened up the greatest opportunity to date for the Kurdish people to establish a new negotiating position with the two governments concerned. The exploitation of such an opportunity depended, however, upon the Kurds on both sides of the border being able to agree a general position and policy. This did not happen, and the Kurds remained divided politically.

In Iraq, PUK had been in a difficult position throughout most of 1983. In addition to its struggle with the Baghdad government, it faced the onslaught of Turkey and Iran. In May 1983 Turkish troops, apparently with Iraqi blessing, crossed the border to attack Kurdish territory. Although this was KDP territory, PUK was alarmed at the danger of the Kurds facing all three regional powers at once. In June and July Iran launched a massive assault on Iraq, including the Kurdish sector where 150,000 of its troops moved against about 15,000 pesh mergas of KDPI and PUK. Its objective was the network of refugee camps near Hajj Umran, housing not only the KDPI headquarters but also about 20,000 women and children. These camps were destroyed and, as already mentioned, PUK's adversary, KDP, installed. A year later the Iranian army was still in the area, increased in strength to about 250,000 along a front from Urumiya to Qasr-i-Shirin.

Fortunately for PUK, the government in Baghdad was also feeling the strain of war in 1983. Baghdad had been increasingly unhappy that PUK and its allies were successfully pinning down up to 50,000 troops needed on the Iranian front. It was also alarmed by the very high rate of desertion amongst Kurds conscripted into the ranks of the Iraqi army. Saddam Hussein himself admitted to 48,000 desertions in January 1983, and in April offered an amnesty to deserters and a promise these would not be sent to the front if they rejoined the army.

Few responded. Both Baghdad and PUK were concerned by Iraq's reverses on the battlefield in Hajj Umran in July, and around Panjwin in October, with the Iraqis fearful that Iran would break through its defences, and the Kurds that they would find themselves having to parley with a victorious Iranian government. Even the Ba'th was preferable to that.

The ceasefire agreement of December 1983

Baghdad and the PUK commenced secret negotiations towards the end of the year. They both badly needed a breathing space. On 10 December 1983 PUK reached an accord with the Ba'th government, an apparent about-face which brought accusations of treachery from PUK's erstwhile allies, particularly the Iraq Communist Party. From PUK's viewpoint, however, the ceasefire offered three things: a breathing space, a possibility for the realization of what PUK considered were Kurdish rights, and time in which to reorganize, failing a successful outcome to negotiations. The immediate effect was to relieve pressure on PUK, with the withdrawal of Iraqi troops from the area (much needed to confront Iran), and with the supply of weapons with which to defend Kurdish areas against Iranian forces.

PUK's demands included:

1. Extension of the autonomous region to include Kirkuk, Mandali, Khanaqin, Jabal Sinjar;
2. A halt to arabization of Kurdish areas, and the return of displaced Kurds;
3. The removal of the *cordon sanitaire* along Iranian and Turkish borders, including strategic hamlets;
4. Clearly established autonomous powers except in foreign affairs, the economy and defence;
5. Members of the executive to be elected by the legislature;
6. Reconstitution of cultural life, with Kurdish as the official language of the region, and establishment of a University of Kurdistan at Sulaymaniya;
7. The formal constitution of the pesh mergas as the force guaranteeing autonomy;
8. Security in the region to be a regional rather than a national responsibility;
9. The allocation of 30% (reduced later to 25%) of oil revenue to the development of Kurdistan.

There were a number of other measures for immediate implementation. These included the release of all political and military prisoners on either side, the dissolution of the so-called *Jash*, that is those Kurdish irregular troops numbering anything between 10,000 and 20,000 troops formed into 'Light Brigades' serving the government. The reason went beyond the question of collaborators. PUK had to ensure that its politicians and pesh mergas alone represented the Kurds, and that it had no Kurdish rival in government, unless these were the result of electoral procedure rather than political alliance with the Ba'th. It therefore also insisted on the removal of Hashim Aqrawi and his pro-governmental (KDP) and also the Kurdish Revolutionary Party from government.

Baghdad agreed to some of these demands and agreed to discuss others. It made an undertaking to release Kurdish detainees and to repatriate Kurds settled elsewhere in the country, to revise the autonomy law in favour of the Kurds, and to extend it to include other areas inhabited by Kurds.

However, it is unlikely that either Talabani or President Saddam Hussein viewed this agreement, and particularly the final undertaking, as much more than a way of gaining time. Baghdad would not agree to ceding Kirkuk. 'Do not insist on Kirkuk being a Kurdish town and we shall not insist on it not being Kurdish,' Saddam Hussein reportedly told Talabani. A mixed administration was agreed to in principle, though it is hard to see how this could ever have worked. Mandali and Khanaqin were too close to Iran and Sinjar to Syria (which had supported PUK militarily and financially) for Baghdad to feel ready to cede them. It was also questionable whether Sinjar was predominantly Kurdish. Hopes that an agreement could be hammered out, however, plummeted in March 1984 with the execution of 24 young Kurds in Sulaymaniya, allegedly for desertion and draft-dodging, and the shooting of a number of students at Arbil University. Talabani's brother, Shaikh Hama Salih, and his two daughters were also killed, allegedly by pro-government forces at about the same time. PUK had already lost 1400 members by execution between 1976 and 1983.

Baghdad had begun to receive considerable external assistance to avoid defeat by Iran from the USA, the USSR and France. It could also count on Turkey in the north, as it had been able to in May 1983, to intervene to control both Iraqi and Turkish Kurds in northern Iran and to protect the oil pipeline from Kirkuk.

It is not surprising, therefore, that hardly any progress was made. On 18 October PUK broke off negotiations. PUK subsequently believed that the Iraqi government was warned by a visiting delegation in

Baghdad led by Foreign Minister Halefoglu three days earlier that an agreement with PUK would lead Turkey (wary of its own Kurds) to close the pipeline and seal the border (thereby virtually bringing Iraq to its knees in its struggle with Iran).

But Turkish intervention in the negotiations, if true, came only as the last straw to dash PUK's hopes. On 20 August 1984 Na'im Haddad, speaker of Iraq's National Assembly, announced that PUK would shortly join the National Front alongside the Ba'th to fight the forthcoming elections. PUK was angry at what it considered an attempt to stampede it when Baghdad had implemented hardly any of the agreement, particularly since it had indicated its willingness to participate in elections only after a definitive agreement had been reached. At that stage agreement had been reached on only about six points, but these had either not been implemented or only partially so.[98]

In addition there were the points which Baghdad had refused to countenance. These included the disbandment of the 'Light Brigades' and 'Saladin Knights' (the Kurdish pro-government irregulars), the dismissal of Hashim Aqrawi and other Kurds in the pro-government National Front (the Ba'th would have been reluctant to ditch Aqrawi and other Kurdish allies of 10 years' standing), and the refusal of 18 October to include Sinjar in the autonomous region. (Baghdad had already successfully fudged Kirkuk, refused Mandali and Khanaqin but accepted Kifra and Aqra within the autonomous area.) There had been one or two clashes towards the end of the summer as it became clear that an agreement was less likely. In September a leading PUK military commander, Sayyid Karim, had been killed in ambush by Kurdish pro-government irregulars.

In retrospect it is most unlikely that PUK seriously believed it would get Sinjar, Kirkuk or Khanaqin. These places were clearly far too sensitive for Baghdad to cede. However, PUK had its own following to consider, and the inevitable accusations from its Kurdish opponents that it was selling the Kurdish birthright for a mess of pottage. It therefore had to appear maximalist, at least until Baghdad showed real promise of compromise on other questions.

After the failure of the talks, two leading members of the government went to parley with Talabani on 18 October to attempt to keep the ceasefire. Talabani's response was a renewal of clashes with local government forces, although it was only in mid-January 1985 that PUK resumed the offensive formally. By February 1985 PUK's 10,000 or so pesh mergas had re-established control of the roads and countryside between Kirkuk and Sulaymaniya, and the land up to the border where it abuts with KDPI-held Hawraman.

KDP's 12,000 or so fighters controlled a swathe of territory from Syria in the west to Rowanduz in the east. One of Iraq's four armies was preoccupied with containing the Kurd revolt, in addition to a reported 50,000 pro-government Kurdish irregulars. In August 1984, 15,000 Iraqi troops failed to dislodge KDP pesh mergas from the area of Zakho and Dohuk. KDP gained from cross-border co-operation and support of Turkish Kurds.

The end of the Iran-Iraq War

The year 1987 had seen the progressive gathering of Kurdish political and military strength, through the rapprochement of the two main parties, the Patriotic Union of Kurdistan (PUK) and the Democratic Party of Iraqi Kurdistan (KDP) in early 1987 and the subsequent formation of the Iraqi Kurdistan Front (IKF) in July 1987, a coalition of the five main Kurdistan nationalist parties waging war against Saddam Hussein's government in Baghdad.[99]

These parties called for the formation of an Iraqi National Front of all opposition parties, the overthrow of Saddam Hussein, an end to the Iran—Iraq conflict on the basis of mutual respect of sovereignty on both sides of the international border, full Kurdish national rights and democratic choice, and the safeguarding of minority rights in Kurdish areas for Turkoman and Assyrian communities. The PUK called for Iraqi recognition of the Kurdish right to self-determination which its leader, Jalal Talabani, hinted would, if recognized, lead to insistence on genuine autonomy rather than secession from the Iraqi State.

At the same time that it formally joined forces with other Kurdish groups, the PUK also abandoned its previous policy of avoiding open co-operation with Iranian forces. This previous policy had been based on two considerations: the dangers implicit in reliance on Tehran in view of the sudden withdrawal of support for the KDP by Iran in March 1975; and the desire to be seen in Iraq as fighting for Kurdish rights but not as helping Iran to defeat Iraq. Together Iranian and PUK troops began to make co-operative inroads into the Iraqi Kurdish mountains. Given PUK's insistence on the principle of self-determination, it was inevitable that militant Kurdish nationalism was seen by Baghdad to be treason at a moment of great national peril.[100] In southern Iraq, Iran consolidated its hold on the Fao peninsula and seemed to inch its way towards Basra.

In mid-April 1987 PUK forces attacked and captured strategic areas east of Sulaymaniya. A week later, joint Kurdish forces, with strong Iranian support, temporarily captured Qaradagh, 25 km south of

Sulaymaniya. A few miles further north, Iranian troops captured over 250 sq. kms of Iraqi Kurdistan in its 'Kerbala 10' offensive. A far wider area was lost to Iraqi control, however, after nightfall, as a result of Kurdish guerrilla operations. In the northern sector, the KDP was able to dominate the area between Zakho and Aqra, and on occasions was able to cut the main road into Turkey. To the south, the PUK dominated an even larger zone, from the Greater Zab river southwards to the Diyala river, just south of Kifri, cutting the main Kirkuk—Baghdad road and ambushing Iraqi convoys trying to use these roads after nightfall. Throughout the area, however, Kurdish forces generally avoided holding towns, and concentrated on tying down Iraqi forces through domination of the countryside and arterial routes. During 1987 two out of Iraq's seven armies were tied down in dealing with the Kurdish threat. In mid-May PUK forces captured the strategic town of Rawanduz in order to protect the population from deportation.

However, Kurdish triumph was tempered by Baghdad's savage reaction to the growing Kurdish and Iranian threat in the northern sector. It had already demonstrated its disregard for civilized norms. In 1983 8000 non-combatant members of the Barzani clan had been arrested and, despite inquiries by Amnesty International, remained unaccounted for and must be presumed dead. In January 1987, at the time that the PUK and KDP were negotiating their alliance, a number of bodies were reported delivered to Sulaymaniya for burial by next of kin. These bodies, it was claimed, were the mutilated remains of some 57 children and youths who had been arrested by the authorities in September 1985.[101]

Chemical weapons and civilian massacre

Baghdad now adopted more drastic measures. In early 1987 the government began a policy of removing all civilians and livestock from swathes of Kurdish countryside, designating these areas 'free fire zones' in which any living creatures – human or otherwise – were to be shot on sight. All areas still under Iraqi control during daylight hours were denuded of their population and their villages razed. This policy covered areas from Zakho in the north across to Halabja in the south and east to Sulaymaniya.

Three thousand or so villages and hamlets were razed, and approximately 500,000 Kurdish civilians were deported to detention camps in the desert areas of south and west Iraq. Many others fled as refugees to Iran. Where villagers were caught returning to their destroyed villages, they were reportedly executed without regard for age or sex. In Kirkuk, which Kurds claimed as a Kurdish city, the government reportedly removed thousands of its Kurd and Turkoman citizens, and replaced them with almost 10,000 Arab families. Jalal Talabani warned that the Iraqi government's objective was the removal of all Kurdish presence in the mountain areas by 1990.[102]

There was another sinister development. When PUK forces made significant advances around Sulaymaniya in April 1987, Baghdad used chemical weapons against a number of Kurdish villages in the battle zone in the period 15-21 April. Although news of these chemical attacks was disseminated internationally, no steps were taken to restrain Iraq. Furthermore, although a UN Commission investigated and confirmed the alleged use of chemical weapons by Iraq against Iran, it did not investigate allegations of their use against Iraqi Kurds, since it was not authorized to do so.

Notwithstanding these events, many Kurds looked forward optimistically at the outset of 1988 to an Iranian and Kurdish victory which would bring about the downfall of Saddam Hussein and the fulfilment of Kurdish demands in Iraq. At first it looked as if such expectations might be fulfilled as Kurdish forces increased their zone of control from roughly 2500 sq. kms in June 1987 to almost 10,700 sq. kms, roughly the size of Lebanon, at the outset of 1988. In January PUK forces captured the summer seat of the Iraq government at Sari Rash, north east of Arbil. On 16 March PUK and Iranian forces captured Halabja, with the immediate prospect of the capture of Darbandikan Dam, followed by a broad thrust down the Diyala river towards Kifri and Khanaqin.

For Baghdad the danger was considerable, and its response was swift. The following day it attacked Halabja with chemical weapons. It is believed that 6350 died in the attack, largely civilians.[103] There were expressions of concern by international leaders, but no steps were taken to restrain Iraq which continued to use gas against civilian as well as military targets in different parts of Kurdistan in April and May.

Meanwhile Iran's capacity to continue its costly war began to collapse. In April, in the extreme south of Iraq, its troops were driven out of Fao and back from Basra. Elsewhere, too, the Iranian forces began to give way. In the first half of July Iranian forces abandoned Halabja and Hajj Umran, its two most important possessions in Iraq. On 22 July it announced that it was willing to accept the internationally accepted basis for a ceasefire, Security Council Resolution 598. On 20 August 1988 the ceasefire came into effect.

Five days later Baghdad initiated an all-out assault on Kurdish nationalist positions, using 60,000 seasoned troops now freed from the war with Iran. Ground forces were supported by air strikes against Kurdish positions. In addition, gas attacks were renewed against villages remaining in IKF-held areas. Baghdad's objectives seem to have included the destruction of Kurdish nationalist forces, and the removal of all inhabitants and livestock from captured areas.

By the end of August over 60,000 Kurdish civilians had fled across the border into Turkey. A similar or greater number fled across the border into Iran. Where possible, Iraqi troops endeavoured to cut the fugitives off. Among those who were captured, many men were separated from their families and were presumed killed.

By the first week of September it was estimated that over 2000 civilians had died, and some claimed that 'tens of thousands' had died. There was no way of verifying such reports. In one case it was reliably reported that 1300 civilians had been ambushed, killed and buried in a mass grave.[104] Women and children seem to have been deported out of Kurdistan to camps elsewhere in Iraq.

The renewed use of chemical weapons led to further international condemnation of Iraq, but no government instigated any penalties against Iraq for its actions. Even after these condemnations, Iraq continued to use chemical weapons with impunity, for example on 11 and 14 October against targets in Kirkuk and Sulaymaniya provinces.[105]

Baghdad's offensive in the last week of August virtually removed all Kurdish nationalist footholds in Iraq. Guerrilla activities continued by small bands of 10 or so men, but there was no prospect of such operations forcing any concession from Saddam Hussein. Furthermore, with much of Kurdistan denuded of its population, it was far harder to sustain guerrilla warfare in the countryside. At the outset of 1989 it seemed likely that the Kurdish national movement would resort to urban guerrilla warfare or terrorism as the only remaining military options. At the end of September 1988 the PUK was in receipt of Syrian aid to continue the struggle against Saddam Hussein, the first such aid from Syria since 1981.

Refugee exodus 1988

Meanwhile, the continuing struggle against Saddam Hussein had resulted in the mass movement of Kurdish civilians: refugees across neighbouring Turkish and Iranian borders, and deportees to detention camps in the deserts of south and west Iraq. By 1987 there were already at least 150,000 Iraqi Kurdish refugees interned in camps in Iran. Of these, perhaps 50,000, had been living in Iran since the collapse of the KDP in 1975, while another 50,000 Shi'i Kurds had been expelled on the grounds of being 'not truly Iraqi' during the late 1970s. The balance were refugees from the war in Kurdistan from 1980 onwards. With Baghdad's onslaught following the Iran—Iraq ceasefire, a massive new wave of refugees took place. An unknown number crossed into Iran. Approximately 60,000 crossed from northern frontier areas into Turkey.

In Iran the longer established refugee communities were confined to two large camps at Karaj, near Tehran, Jahrurn in Shiraz province, and a smaller camp at Khurram Abad. Conditions have been physically deprived and restricted, with strictly limited time allowed outside camp, and inadequate food and health facilities inside. Like Turkey, Iran was extremely reluctant to allow foreign aid workers into its camps, although both UNHCR and ICRC achieved limited access. Until 1988 some Kurdish civilians found the conditions in these camps so bad that they preferred to risk the dangers of returning to the war zone in Iraqi Kurdistan. Those Kurds transferred from Turkey in September and October 1988 were moved into inadequate tented camps near Khoi, Urumiya and Ushnaviya (which housed a total of about 46,000 refugees), on the western side of Lake Urumiya.

When Iraq offered all Iraqi Kurds, with the exception of Jalal Talabani, an amnesty on 6 September 1988, virtually none of the refugees accepted it. Both Kurds and international organizations viewed it as an untrustworthy offer in view of previous Iraqi behaviour.

13

KURDISH UPRISING 1991
– BRIEF VICTORY AND BITTER DEFEAT

Kurdish reassessment

The rapid defeat of the Kurdistan Front in August 1988, and the stringent resettlement and depopulation measures taken by Baghdad, which left the Kurdish people present on only 10,000 of Iraqi Kurdistan's 74,000 sq. km., inevitably demanded a major reassessment by the Kurdish leadership of the tactics that had been used.

The Kurdish armed struggle since 1974 had proved highly counter-productive. With hindsight, it was possible to argue that had the Kurdish leadership accepted the Autonomy Law in 1974, even as a incomplete symbol for the real substance, approximately 4000 villages and farmsteads would still be inhabited, and Kurdish culture would still be flourishing in their mountains of Kurdistan.

It was natural that the Kurdish parties underwent a period of self-doubt and self-criticism. Halabja was seen by some as a massive blunder for which the Kurdistan Front was itself partly responsible. It should, in their view, never have let the Iranian Pasdaran forces enter the area, for this sent the wrong message to Baghdad. At the 10th National Congress of the KDP, in December 1989, it was accepted that the assumption that Saddam's regime would collapse in the course of war with Iran had been misplaced.

It was also recognized that the type of war which had been success-fully waged in the 1960s was no longer possible. While the use of ter-rorism was absolutely rejected by Mas'ud Barzani, it was decided to relaunch guerrilla attacks by small teams, in such a way as to make it difficult for reprisals to be taken against the civilian population. Similar conclusions were drawn by the PUK leadership. 'The decision is that the struggle must continue', remarked Jalal Talabani[106]. The PUK was able to maintain small bases on the very edges of Iraq Kurdistan, too close to Iran to be feasible for Baghdad to attack.

Both the KDP and PUK also made a major new diplomatic effort to win friends in the Arab world and the west. In the past they had been frequently rebuffed, but several Arab states were increasingly uneasy about Saddam Hussein. Talabani had little difficulty in establishing cordial relations with Egypt, Syria, Saudi, Libya, and South Yemen. Algeria was more cautious, since it recognized a similarity between Baghdad's difficulties with the Kurds and its problems with its own minority Berber population.

It might be thought that Saddam was sufficiently strong that he had no interest in making peace with the Kurdish opposition. In fact he was anxious to do so because he believed the Kurds were ready to settle on his terms. On 6 September 1988 Saddam Hussein announced the first of six amnesties, the last of which was declared on 11 June 1990, only eight weeks before he invaded Kuwait. In spite of the privations in the Turkish camps, no more than about 2000 Kurds responded to these offers. The subsequent disappearance of some of these returnees and the poisoning incidents in the refugee camps in Turkey discouraged others.

Saddam also made indirect contact with the Kurdish leadership, through Mukarem Talabani who met Jalal (they are unrelated) in Moscow. But the Kurdish leadership felt threatened by an apparent coincidence of attitude concerning the Kurds in Baghdad and Tehran. Indeed, in June 1990 Mas'ud Barzani returned from top level meetings in Tehran reporting Iranian and Iraqi unease at Kurdish diplomatic efforts in the Arab world and in Europe.

The defeat of 1988, however, did not produce greater willingness to negotiate with Baghdad. The Kurdistan Front concluded that negotiation could not seriously take place until Saddam himself had been replaced. Since their objectives seemed further away than ever before, a number of Kurdish leaders began to talk in vague terms beyond the idea of autonomy. Some spoke ambiguously of Kurdish 'self-determination', refusing to be drawn on whether this might actually mean more than autonomy. Others, like Talabani, spoke warmly of a federal solution to Iraq's ethnic and religious divides, citing what proved to be an unfortunate example, Yugoslavia.

The invasion of Kuwait and the Gulf War

Saddam Hussein's invasion of Kuwait in August 1990, put the Kurdish leadership in a dilemma. Some believed they should strike a deal with Saddam since he could ill afford the opening of a northern front, and he needed to free the eight divisions deployed in Kurdistan for use elsewhere. But the predominant view was that he could not be trusted, it would be unpopular among ordinary Kurds who had suffered at Saddam's hands, and that it would be unwise for the Kurds to be associated with him at a time when he faced almost unanimous international condemnation.

On the other hand there were dangers in openly siding with the United States and its allies. Jalal Talabani went to Washington in mid-August but the State department refused to see him. The KDP viewed his move as a mistake[107] and its spokesman in London said that in any case the Kurds did not trust the United States. Nevertheless, the KDP continued to provide intelligence information to the Coalition, despite the latter's apparent disregard of the Coalition for the material it offered concerning the whereabouts of the foreign hostages Iraq had seized.

Meanwhile the Kurdistan Front prepared for the chance of a power vacuum in Baghdad in the event of war between Baghdad and the Coalition. In Kurdistan itself, the reduction of government forces gave pesh merga forces greater freedom of movement to the extent that they could even enter Dohuk. The Front met with Turkish and Iranian Kurdish leaders in order to co-ordinate and maximize the support in any fight that might develop with the Iraqi army.

Kurdish leaders also sought meetings with European governments, most notably the French administration,[108] in order to reassure them that they were wholly opposed to the fragmentation of Iraq and wished Kurdistan to remain an integral part of it. This was important because of President Özal's presumed insistence that Turkey would only join the Coalition on condition that no separate Kurdish entity would emerge as a result of the crisis.

Finally, as the probability of war and the possibility of internal Iraqi collapse increased, the Kurdistan Front negotiated with other opposition groups in order to present a credible alternative to the Ba'thist regime. On 27 December 1990 an agreement was announced in Damascus by 17 Iraqi opposition groups, including the Kurdistan Front.[109] In spite of their disparate ideologies, they were able to agree on the overthrow of Saddam Hussein, the introduction of democratic reform, respect for human rights, and political pluralism. With regard to the Kurds they all accepted the principle of Kurdish autonomy.

However, this opposition was unable to gain the serious attention of the Coalition.[110] The latter feared the fragmentation of Iraq, which it thought likely if an untried and loose group of opposition parties assumed power. The US also feared Shi'i ambitions, still paranoid a decade after the US hostage crisis in Tehran. It found difficulty in differentiating between Iranian, Lebanese and Iraqi Shi'is. It had also (pre-

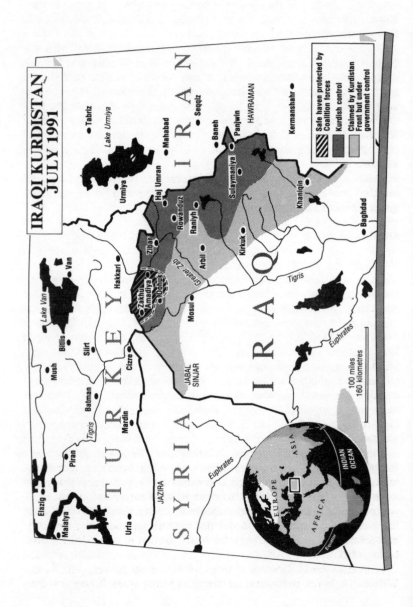

sumably) assured Turkey it would not allow a Kurdish entity to be established in the north. Finally, its ideal postwar scenario was a coup d'état by one of Saddam's generals, ensuring the best prospect (in US eyes) for the continued stability of Iraq.

When the Coalition actually launched its ground forces against Iraqi positions in Kuwait in January 1991, the Kurdistan Front was still tying down substantial government forces, and was in a position to seize the towns of Kurdistan. Furthermore, the Front's supporters had persuaded large numbers of the (officially) 100,000 strong 'Light Regiments' (*Jash*) that in the case of an Iraqi collapse they would be welcomed into the Kurdistan Front's ranks. All that the Front lacked – but it was to prove critical – was the assurance that the Coalition would be sympathetic to a Kurdish rising, and to the establishment of a democratic regime in Baghdad. Neither Jalal Talabani in Washington at the beginning of March 1991, nor Hoshyar Zibari, KDP representative in Europe, was given access to US State Department officials.

Kurdish uprising

No sooner had the Coalition routed Iraqi forces on the battlefield than Shi'is in southern Iraq, encouraged by army deserters, rose in revolt. For two weeks it seemed as if Baghdad might be unable to restore its authority. The Kurdish leadership treated events in the south with caution.

But on 4 March a spontaneous popular rising in the Kurdish town of Ranya spread like wildfire across Kurdistan, obliging the Kurdistan Front to throw its pesh mergas into the fray. One town after another fell rapidly to the Kurdish forces. Thousands of Iraqi troops surrendered, many joining the Kurdish rising. The jash, which proved far less numerous than officially stated, defected en masse. Very few remained loyal to Baghdad. By 19 March virtually all Kurdistan including Kirkuk, had fallen to the Kurdish insurgents.

The Kurdish triumph proved shortlived. On 28 March government forces mounted their counter- offensive, using helicopter gunships, tanks, multiple rocket launchers and heavy artillery. In spite of appeals from the Kurdish leadership, US President Bush refused to intervene. It was generally believed in Iraqi opposition circles that Bush was doing the bidding of Turkey, which did not wish to see the Kurds triumph, and Saudi Arabia, which feared the establishment of a part-Shi'i regime in Baghdad.

Within 48 hours Kirkuk was once more in Iraqi government hands. Within 72 hours thousands of terrified Kurds were fleeing towards

Turkey and Iran, as the other towns of Kurdistan fell one after another to government forces. On 2 April the city of Sulaymaniya was captured.

The establishment of 'safe havens'

By 3 April hundreds of thousands of Kurdish asylum-seekers had reached the Turkish border, in cars, taxis, trucks, tractors or on foot. In spite of the bitter winter conditions and air attacks on the fugitives, Turkish troops prevented them from crossing to safety. 'We cannot let them cross in,' announced a Foreign Ministry spokesman. 'There are 250,000 of them.'[111]

Amid a rising public outcry at the suffering of the Kurdish people, the UN Security Council finally passed Resolution 688 on 5 April calling on the government to refrain from its attacks on the Kurdish population, and to allow the provision of international aid. On 8 April UK Prime Minister John Major urged the establishment of an enclave for the Kurds, taking up on a proposal made a week earlier by President Özal in order to relieve the international pressure on Turkey to let Kurdish asylum-seekers cross the border. Initially Mr Major proposed that the towns of Kurdistan should be included, creating the impression that a Kurdish autonomous region might be created under international protection. During the next week, this proposal was reduced to a 'safe haven' – the protection of Kurds in a smaller area stretching from Zakho to Amadiya, and reaching almost as far south as Dohuk.

In the meantime a major relief exercise was undertaken, primarily by Coalition armed forces and by non-governmental agencies (NGOs) in order to bring succour to those dying or starving on the Turkish border or in Iran. By this time there were an estimated 400,000 asylum seekers on Turkey's border, and over one million who had crossed into Iran, out of whom some estimated that roughly 1000 were dying daily on each frontier.[112]

By 17 April Coalition forces had entered northern Iraq to establish camp areas for Kurds stranded on the Turkish border. On 19 April Iraq reluctantly agreed to UN 'humanitarian centres' in Iraq to monitor the security of the civilian population and to organize the distribution of aid. Iraq's decision to agree to the UN deployment was motivated by the hope that the presence of the Coalition forces would be of short duration. But it was 27 April before the first refugees returned to Iraq under the safe havens plan,[113] and the first week of June before all those on the Turkish border had entered either the safe havens or the still 'liberated' zone further east. By this time only 300,000 or so of the

1.2 million refugees inside Iran had actually returned. Most decided to wait and see what became of the Kurdistan Front's negotiations with Baghdad.

These negotiations between the Kurdish leadership and Saddam Hussein began officially on 18 April, but in fact messages had been passing between the two for some time. Mas'ud Barzani had given the first indication that he was willing to negotiate a compromise with Saddam Hussein before the end of March.[114]

The Kurdistan Front decided on talks because of the unprecedented human tragedy which had befallen the Iraqi Kurdish people, and because of the clear unwillingness of the Coalition to support the Kurds and Shi'a in their attempt to bring about the overthrow of Saddam Hussein. They also hoped they would be able to exploit the presence of Coalition forces in northern Iraq, and the continued application of sanctions against Baghdad in order to elicit the kind of autonomy agreement they had hoped for in 1974. They were, however, aware that their decision was extremely damaging to the Opposition parties, since the overthrow of Saddam was the basis of their unity.

On 24 April an agreement in principle was struck between the Kurdish leadership and Baghdad which affirmed the principle of democracy in Iraq, freedom of the press, and allowing the creation of an autonomous region in which Kurds could return to the towns and villages destroyed in 1987-88. But Baghdad demurred at their demand for Kirkuk to replace Arbil as capital, and for the autonomous region to run from Sinjar (west of Mosul) as far south as Khaniqin, at international guarantees, and at the idea of free elections followed by the writing of a new constitution. Once again, as in 1970-74, the Kurds discovered that an agreement in principle was far easier to obtain than a satisfactory agreement in detail.

When Coalition forces began to withdraw from the safe haven areas at the beginning of June, the Kurds had reason to believe that Saddam Hussein was delaying a final agreement in the hope that the Kurds would lose their international protection. Throughout May there had been repeated statements from the Kurdish leadership that the signing of an agreement was imminent. Yet those details of the talks which did emerge indicated that the number of sticking points were increasing rather than decreasing. Baghdad would not accept Kirkuk as the capital of autonomous Kurdistan, would not accept international involvement in the autonomy agreement, and would not agree to rewriting a new constitution already drafted by the Ba'th.

By early June it seemed that Saddam Hussein was delaying an agreement, in the hope that the Coalition handover to UN observers and its withdrawal from northern Iraq would leave the Kurds in a weak negotiating position. It was becoming equally clear to Britain and its European allies that American haste to withdraw its troops (on 18 June the US government announced that its already reduced force in northern Iraq would be completely withdrawn by the end of June) was undermining the very stability and sense of security in northern Iraq necessary to permit their withdrawal.

Much of the impetus for abandoning the decision to withdraw completely came from service personnel in the field. They recognized the danger that a premature withdrawal without an adequate protection force (the UN had by this time recruited only 50 of its projected 500 UN observer force) risked a second mass flight to the Turkish and Iranian borders.[115] On 21 June the US government agreed to keep some troops close to north Iraq and announced that withdrawal had been indefinitely postponed.

Meanwhile, the Kurdish leadership rejected the autonomy agreement negotiated by Mas'ud Barzani in Baghdad. Although the projected deal offered the Kurds political and military control over the three provinces of Dohuk, Arbil and Sulaymaniya, and the restoration of villages destroyed since the 1970s, the Front decided it was unable to accept the terms offered. In particular it could not undertake the requirements to cut all links with allies both inside and outside Iraq, to hand over heavy weapons and to suspend the Front's two broadcasting services. Baghdad's offer of elections and a multi-party system for the whole of Iraq was also considered inadequate and unconvincing. Talks were resumed in early July with repeated announcements of the 'imminence' of an accord.

On 15 July the Coalition Forces completed their withdrawal from northern Iraq, leaving the safety of the Kurds and the chances for a autonomy agreement largely dependent upon the seriousness with which Baghdad treated the deterrent force (Operation Poised Hammer) stationed in Turkey, and the prospect of indefinite sanctions.

In any case, any autonomy agreement achieved between Baghdad and the Kurdistan Front depends in the creation of a relationship of trust between Baghdad and the Kurdish and other peoples of Iraq. That relationship remains as distant as ever without a fundamental constitutional reform of the State which will replace the Ba'th dictatorship with representative government.

14

KURDS ON THE PERIPHERY
– SYRIA, LEBANON AND USSR[116]

There are large Kurdish communities outside the central mountainous of Kurdistan. The main concentrations are in Syria, Lebanon and the USSR.

The Kurds in Syria

The Kurds in Syria number about 8% of the total population. They are found in three main areas, in Kurd Dagh, the rugged hill country in the north-west of Aleppo, in north-west Jazira (the 'island' between the Tigris and Euphrates) around Jarablus and Ain al Arab, also against the Turkish border, and thirdly in their largest concentration in northern Jazira, around Qamishli and in the 'beak' of north-eastern Syria against the borders of Iraq and Turkey.

The inhabitants of Kurd Dagh and some in the Jarablus area have been living there for centuries. These, and smaller groups dating back to the medieval military 'camps' of Kurdish troops, in Damascus and elsewhere,[117] have virtually no long-standing relations with the Kurds of Iraq or Turkey. Although they may still speak Kurdish, many are either half or wholly 'arabicized', that is, they feel they belong now to the local Arab culture.

The largest community, in north Jazira, is formed of those who became permanently settled inside Syria's borders following the collapse of the Ottoman Empire. A relatively small number of these had traditionally used northern Jazira as winter pasture, driving their livestock down from the anti-Taurus mountain range each autumn. They shared this area with Arab nomadic tribes, notably the Shammar, who also used the area during summer, when driven northwards by the heat and absence of grazing further south.

The overwhelming proportion, however, were Kurds fleeing from Turkey in the years after 1920, and particularly after the collapse of Shaikh Said of Piran's revolt and the subsequent risings. These settled what was a relatively uninhabited and fertile area. It is amongst these Kurds that national awareness and tensions with the Arab majority in Syria have been most felt.

During the 1920s refugee Kurdish aghas from Anatolia continued to raid to and fro across the Syrian-Turkish border. The presence of a considerable number of Christians – mainly Assyrian and Armenian refugees from Anatolia, who hoped for relative freedom from Muslim rule in Damascus – contributed to tension, particularly since the French mandatory authorities encouraged minority separatism in Syria. The French made a practice of recruiting minorities, including the Kurds, into their local force, *les troupes spéciales du Levant*. They also encouraged the Kurd nationalist party, *Khoybun*, thus giving Arab nationalists a cause for unease. During the 1930s Kurds maintained an ambivalent attitude toward both Muslim Arab Damascus and their Christian neighbours.

Following effective Syrian independence in 1945, the tension between Arabs and Kurds was initially concerned neither with separatism nor with minority persecution. On the contrary, the first three military coups in Syria, all in 1949, were carried out by officers with part-Kurd backgrounds. All of these relied on officers of similar ethnic background. Some Arabs felt such behaviour was an undesirable carry-over from Kurdish participation in *les troupes spéciales*. Following Shishakli's fall in 1954 it is said that high-ranking Kurds were purged from the army, and certainly by 1958 this was so.

The union of Syria and Egypt in the United Arab Republic in 1958 triggered the first round of oppressive behaviour towards the Kurds. This was partly because of the intensity of Arabism following Nasser's triumphal first years in Egypt. It was also because some Kurdish intellectuals had founded the Kurdish Democratic Party of Syria a few months earlier. This called for recognition of the Kurds as an ethnic group and for democratic government in Damascus, drawing attention to the lack of economic development for Kurdish areas, and also to the fact that the police and military academies were closed to Kurdish applicants. Psychologically the timing could hardly have been worse. Those caught with Kurdish gramophone records or publications, which had hitherto been tolerated, saw them seized and destroyed, and were themselves put into prison. In August 1960 the authorities arrested a number of the new KDP leadership and 5000 'suspects'.

The question of ethnic and religious identity has bedevilled the development of political parties in Syria. Pressure on the Kurds intensified after the collapse of the union with Egypt in 1961. That year a census was carried out in Jazira as a result of which 120,000 Kurds were discounted as foreigners. The following year a plan to create an 'Arab belt' 10—15km deep along the border of Jazira began to be implemented, but was changed to one of establishing model farms, staffed by Arabs. Although these plans were never fully implemented, they caused enough concern and distress for up to 60,000 Kurds to leave the area for Damascus, Turkey and mainly for Lebanon, where they found work during the 1960s' building boom. Like Christians in Iraq who find themselves without full citizenship, those Kurds stripped of nationality still found themselves required to serve in the Syrian army.

There was no relief from persecution when the Ba'th assumed power in 1963. This was partly on account of the Kurdish revolt against Baghdad, and fears of the infection spreading. The Ba'th launched an absurd publicity campaign to 'save the Jazira from becoming a second Israel', a manifestly unconvincing slogan. Some Kurds were actually expelled, in addition to those already stripped of nationality, and the state refused to implement land reforms where the beneficiaries were Kurdish rather than Arab peasantry. There was also a sense of solidarity between the Ba'th in Baghdad and in Damascus before they split in 1966. The Syrian Ba'th had already demonstrated its distrust of Kurds. When it had merged with the Arab Socialist Party a decade earlier, it had denied membership of the new party to Kurdish peasant members of the ASP. This may well have been partly because of the Hashemite Amir Abdullah's intrigues amongst the Syrian minorities, including the Kurds, in the late 1940s.

It should not be thought that the Ba'th, or the Arabs, were alone in such behaviour. The Kurds themselves were considerably responsible for the failure of the Syrian Communist Party to attract a wider following. It was led for many years by the remarkable Khalid Baqdash, and dominated by other Kurds. One party member commented bitterly on the 'narrow nationalist chauvinism' of the party.[118] As for the KDPS, it broke up under the hostile pressure of government. Repeated arrests of its members and alleged torture had a divisive affect. Although it continued to struggle on, it has never achieved a wide following, and its different factions reflect personality or localist clashes more than any ideological difference.

Ba'th persecution of the Kurds began to ease from 1967 onwards. In 1971 it implemented those land reforms in Kurdish areas already effected elsewhere. However, it was not until 1976 that President Hafiz al Asad officially renounced the long-standing plan to transfer Kurdish and Arab populations in this sensitive area, a leftover from the 'Arab Belt' policy of a decade earlier. Arabs already moved into predominantly Kurdish areas were allowed to stay, but the programme as such was halted. During the mid-1980s the Kurds had felt safer than they had done since the 1950s.

But towards the end of the 1980s there were fears that the period of relaxation was over. Many Kurds continued to be denied citizenship, an ID card or passport. The Kurdish language and culture continued to be prohibited, and Kurdish place names were replaced by Arab ones. Kurds believe discrimination on ethnic grounds continues.[119] Certainly the sense of Kurdish identity grows as Kurds who have been integrated into Arab society for generations rediscover their ethnic origins.

It is difficult in a totalitarian state to measure the rights and freedoms for one particular minority community as distinct from the general restriction on freedoms for the country as a whole. It is thus difficult to evaluate the election of fifteen Kurds as members of the Syrian parliament in 1991, particularly since there is no real democratic process in Syria.

The Kurds in Lebanon

Until the Civil War of 1975-91, there were about 70,000 Kurds living in Lebanon. The overwhelming majority hail from Mardin in southeast Anatolia. The earliest arrivals, during the French mandate, numbered about 15,000. These secured Lebanese citizenship. Since 1961 a few thousand more had residence permits which indicated that the question of citizenship was 'under study'. The majority of Kurds, however, have no permit at all. They arrived to participate in the building boom, because they could earn more than in Syria.

Both socially and economically the Kurds in Lebanon have been in a weak position, carrying out unskilled manual labour for which they have been ill-paid, and unable to press for better conditions for fear of deportation. Since the Civil War began, the Kurds have been amongst the most oppressed. They, together with other Syrians and Shi'ites from south Lebanon, caught the first round of Phalangist fury in the sack of Qarantina and of Naba'. Some were massacred, others fled and since then have led a twilight existence in the beach slums of St Michel and Ouzai, south Beirut. Almost certainly the number of Kurds has dropped by at least 10,000 and possibly by a good deal more, as Kurds have drifted back to Syria on account of the bleak outlook in Lebanon.

The Kurds in the USSR[120]

Although there are no Kurdish territories in the USSR, there are a number of compact Kurdish settlements. According to the 1970 census, there were about 40,000 Kurds in Armenia, and another 21,000 Kurds in Georgia, mainly in Tiblisi, which has a Kurdish quarter. The Kurds of these two areas are mainly Yazidis who moved there to escape persecution in Sinjar and Shaikhan. In Azerbaijan the Kurds number about 150,000, whilst there are at least 50,000 in the Turkoman Republic. There are a few thousand Kurds in Kirghizia and Kazakhstan also.

There are historical reasons for the wide dispersion of Soviet Kurds. A number of Kurdish tribes migrated into the Caucasus region in the second part of the 18th Century, whilst those in Central Asia arrived as a result of their use by the Persian Shahs in the 16th Century to guard their eastern border. The Kurds of Kirghizia and Kazakhstan were forcibly deported from the Caucasus (Georgia and Armenia) in 1937-38 for provoking frontier incidents.

Even before *glasnost* there was a measure of cultural freedom for Kurds: they were allowed their own schools, school books and press. A radio station broadcasts in Kurdish to the whole of Kurdistan. There is a strong sense of identity amongst some Kurds with those elsewhere, and this would seem to override ideological considerations, as exemplified in the remark made by one Kurd:

> *'we know that Barzani is no revolutionary, that he is in fact more of a conservative, but for us he is a symbol, symbol of our Kurdishness. When people come in they can see that we are Kurds [a picture of Barzani hangs on the wall]. During your stay here you must have been told that when the Kurdish uprising collapsed in Iraq, everybody in our community went into mourning.'*[121]

The Kurds are a very small minority in USSR, one of the 100 nationalities recognized. Allowing them cultural freedom in no way threatens the state. Would the state be so tolerant if they were as large a percentage as in Iran, Iraq or Turkey, particularly if (as they are not) they were contiguous with other large concentrations of Kurds over the border?

Glasnost has contributed to a resurgence of Kurdish identity and expression, and a recognition of repression during the Stalin years. At the 28th Congress of the Communist Party in September 1989, a resolution promised:

> *'to take every measure in order to solve the problems of the Crimean*

125

Tartars, Soviet Germans, Greeks, Kurds, Meskhetian Turks and others'.[122]

At the end of 1989 the Supreme Soviet adopted a resolution admitting illegal and repressive acts including forcible resettlement of 12 nationalities in USSR, among them the Kurds. The decision of the 28th Congress to restore the constitutional rights of these deported peoples, in particular to return those who wished it to their place of origin, has not been fulfilled. Nor is there any prospect of fulfilment while the USSR and its constituent republics remain in ferment.

In the meantime, the rise of nationalism resulted in further evictions, this time by nationalists in the different republics in which Kurds find themselves. For example, the conflict between Armenia and Azerbaijan since 1988 has resulted in the eviction of an estimated 18,000 Kurds from Armenia on the grounds that they are Muslim.[123] Efforts have been made in both Armenia and Georgia (both overwhelmingly Christian republics) to divide Yezidis from Muslim Kurds.[124]

However, Kurds themselves have also been affected by the resurgence in national expression in the USSR. They proudly point out that in three (Armenia, Georgia and Azerbaijan) of the nine republics among which they are scattered, there are regular cultural activities and publications.

Reawakened national awareness has resulted in more Soviet citizens declaring themselves to be Kurds.

In 1920 there may have been as many as 500,000 Kurds living in the USSR,[125] although this is probably an exaggeration. Certainly there were well over 100,000 in the mid-1920s, of whom 60,000 were in the then-autonomous Kurdish district of Armenia and over 40,000 in Azerbaijan. But these numbers fell as a result of a programme of assimilation. In the 1939 census Kurds in Azerbaijan had dropped to 6000, and by 1959 to 1500.[126] In the censuses for 1979 and 1989, no Kurds were reported as living in Azerbaijan. According to the 1989 census, there were only 153,000 Kurds living in the USSR, but according to a Kurdish estimate in 1985 there were at least 400,000 Kurds.[127]

If nationalism continues to grow in importance for the Soviet peoples, the number of those defining themselves as Kurds may increase, as hitherto assimilated Kurds rediscover their ethnic origin.

CONCLUSION

ENSURING A KURDISH FUTURE
– THE INTERNATIONAL CHALLENGE

The refugees, displaced and deportees, Iraq's use of chemical warfare, the accusation of genocide, and the continuing political problems posed by the Kurdish question present specific challenges to the international community.

The refugee, displaced and deportee problems.

In spring 1991, approximately one and a half million Kurds fled their homes. Technically, those who did not succeed in entering Turkey were 'displaced' rather than refugee. The numbers of refugee and displaced Kurds was unprecedented, but came as a climax to the repeated flight of Kurds from Iraqi Kurdistan.

In Turkey thousands of Kurds have been forcibly removed from their homes. Some have been resettled elsewhere, others have had to find somewhere to survive. Many have fled to western Europe. If these are often considered to be economic migrants, it is in part because the denial Kurds suffer has both a political and an economic dimension.

There should be fundamental international requirements regarding all refugees. International access to register refugee populations and ensure reasonable conditions of life should be assured. UN Resolution 688 authorized international humanitarian intervention on behalf of the Kurdish people in Iraq. It was a precedent. The principle must be widened to other countries and contexts, to protect both Kurds in other countries suffering state brutality and other threatened groups of people.

The protection of asylum-seekers should be assured until their case has been properly heard and a formal decision made concerning their status. This applies as much to Turkey refusing access to 400,000 Kurds, as to members of the European Community trying to seal its borders against people claiming asylum but accused, in the media and by government authorities, of being economic refugees before their cases have been heard. There is an urgent need for stronger UN involvement in the protection of all asylum-seekers and refugees.

The habitat of the Kurds and other threatened groups must be protected. The deliberate razing of villages and other inhabited locations must be proscribed as a means of defeating guerrilla organizations. In neither Turkey nor Iraq has it succeeded in its stated aim of achieving security. On the contrary, it spreads dissidence, and destroys cultures and societies.

Chemical warfare

The use of chemical weapons against the Kurds is the most serious violation of the 1925 Geneva Protocol, prohibiting the use of such weapons, since Mussolini's invasion of Abyssinia in 1935. Iraq has resolutely denied the use of chemical weapons against its Kurdish citizens. However, it admitted using chemical weapons against Iranian forces and the evidence of their use against the Kurds in 1987 and 1988 is overwhelming.

With regard to the Kurdish population the evidence is as follows:[128]

a) Physical evidence of survivors of gas attacks show classic symptoms of mustard gas poisoning: blurry vision, difficulty in breathing, vomiting and itchy skin;

b) Many animals died in circumstances suggestive of chemical attack. For example, horses brought into Turkey by refugees, and reportedly exposed to chemical weapons, died within a few days. Turkish bee-keepers in border areas reported the sudden death of their swarms after chemical attacks were alleged in late August 1988, deaths so sudden that known natural causes were ruled out. In the border district of Semdinli, honey production fell from 250 tons in 1987 to less than 10 tons in 1988.

c) Iraqi military communications intercepted by US monitoring indicated the use of chemical weapons against the Kurds in late August 1988;[129]

d) Eyewitness accounts of survivors provided constant and accurate descriptions of chemical weapons attacks and their effects. The Senate Foreign Relations Committee report of 21 September 1988 related:

'The refugee accounts we recorded described the attacks on more than 30 different villages... when we found survivors of attacks at different refugee camps in Turkey the descriptions were essentially identical... To dismiss the eyewitness accounts... would require one to believe that 65,000 Kurdish refugees confined to five disparate locations were able to organize a conspiracy in 15 days to defame Iraq and that these refugees were also able to keep their conspiracy a secret...'

Iraq only had to invite independent expert observers to visit every alleged site if it wished to disprove such a conspiracy. This it refused to allow. However, a British journalist, Gwynne Roberts, visited the site of one alleged attack in October 1988 and retrieved a soil sample. On analysis this revealed the presence of dithiane, used in the production of mustard gas.[130] The Senate Foreign Relations Committee concluded that the evidence was overwhelming.

A number of governments condemned Iraq but by the end of 1988 not one had applied any material penalty. The United States administration had condemned Iraq's use of chemical weapons in 1984, but it took no material action. In September 1988 the Senate proposed the enactment of a bill imposing mandatory economic sanctions against Iraq. However, the draft of the bill failed to be enacted as a result of a number of political and administrative factors, including the question of US agricultural credits for Iraq, in which US farmers had a strong interest. The Senate failed to review its efforts in 1989.

In early June 1988 the UK Foreign Secretary called for automatic international investigation whenever a state was accused of using chemical weapons.[131] Britain took a leading role in drafting United Nations Security Council Resolution (UNSCR) 620, unanimously passed on 26 August, condemning the use of chemical weapons and calling for 'appropriate and effective measures' if they were used again. They were used 48 hours after the Resolution, and again in September and October but no appropriate and effective measures were forthcoming.

In October an official British statement spoke of 'compelling indications' of Iraq's use of chemical weapons.[132] Britain reprimanded Iraq verbally. But its actions belied its words. In November its annual export credit facility to Iraq fell due for renewal, a timely opportunity to demonstrate its willingness to apply material penalties. Instead it doubled the amount of its export credit facility to Iraq,[133] creating the impression that, despite its authorship of UNSCR 620, it considered its political and trade relations with Iraq and its Gulf neighbours of greater consequence than the danger of proliferation of the manufacture and use of chemical weapons.

The UK's European partners, who also looked forward to lucrative reconstruction contracts in Iraq, behaved similarly. It was not surprising therefore that when in November 1988 the UN Secretary-General criticized the international community for its abandonment of the Iraqi Kurds, he singled out the UK, France and the Federal Republic of Germany as countries which could have acted more strongly and decisively.[134]

However, it was only in the aftermath of Iraq's defeat by Coalition forces, and the UN's subsequent demands on Iraq, that the full extent of its chemical and biological weapons stockpile was revealed. The role played by both Western and Soviet bloc nations in the supply of conventional weapons and of the components of chemical warfare needs further investigation, followed by resolute international action to deter any repetition elsewhere.

If Iraq's violation of the 1925 Geneva Protocol goes unpunished, other countries will be tempted to act similarly. Moreover, the Security Council will bring its authority into disrepute if it fails to implement its call for appropriate and effective measures against Iraq. The survivors of Iraqi chemical warfare must receive appropriate medical treatment to relieve as far as possible the injuries and illnesses resulting from gas attacks, together with monetary compensation.

There must also be effective international action to stop the manufacture of chemical and biological weapons, including the export of components used in the manufacture of such weapons. Governments must be challenged to put the rule of international law above commercial considerations.

The accusation of genocide

The term 'genocide' is an emotive one, usually associated with the destruction of a whole people. In the Convention on Genocide of 9 December 1948:

'genocide means any of the following acts committed with intent to destroy, in whole or in part, a national, ethnical, racial or religious group, as such:

(a) Killing members of the group;

(b) Causing serious bodily or mental harm to members of the group;

(c) Deliberately inflicting on the group conditions of life calculated to

bring about its physical destruction in whole or in part;

(d) Imposing measures intended to prevent births within the group;

(e) Forcibly transferring children of the group to another group.'

With regard to the Kurds, the use of chemical weapons against civilian targets and the systematic destruction of all life in large swathes of Kurdistan arguably falls within the purview of clause (a). Furthermore, the systematic deportation of the Kurdish people from these areas to non-Kurdish areas of Iraq, the razing of possibly over 3000 of the approximately 4000 villages and hamlets of Kurdistan, and the alleged conversion of most of Kurdistan into a wasteland, through the destruction of forestry and agriculture in the region appears to be a convincing case of clauses (b) and (c).

The Contracting Parties to the Convention undertook to prevent and to punish the crime of genocide. Those familiar with previous cases of genocide will be aware of how difficult it is to obtain implementation of the convention. It requires a Contracting Party, a government or governments, to assemble the evidence and bring a case. In addition, governments follow double standards with regard to human rights and are frequently unwilling to punish genocide if they feel that it may cost them severely in trade, commercial or military terms.

Yet the Genocide Convention is one of the basic instruments of international civilized behaviour. If the international community fails to put the Genocide Convention to the test, the cost is the validity of the Convention itself. Governments may only be prepared to act if there is a sufficient public protest when mass killings go unpunished.

A political solution to the Kurdish question.

It might be argued that the Kurdish people, now over 20 million strong, have the right to self- determination in a state of their own. In theory, such a right can hardly be denied. At a pragmatic level, however, it is impossible to imagine the United Nations, the great powers or the regional states in which the Kurds live considering, even for a moment, such an option. The potential for continuing instability would be considerable. Even were the states of the region to agree on a Kurdish state in their midst, they would find themselves competing for its support in regional disputes. As a landlocked entity, it would be highly susceptible to such pressures.

The Kurds themselves are some way from thinking and operating as one people. They have not yet succeeded in creating a pan-Kurdish national movement, and show little sign of doing so. Iraqi Kurds have travelled furthest in producing a Front, yet the Iraqi Kurdish population is smaller than that of either Turkey or Iran. Moreover it is questionable whether the majority of the Kurdish people would welcome an independent state. It must be borne in mind that several million Kurds earn their living outside Kurdistan, in the towns and cities of the Middle East.

As a consequence the economic wellbeing of probably one third of the Kurdish people depends on an intimate relationship with wider societies and cultures in the region. The interdependence which already existed at the beginning of the 20th Century has increased rather than diminished. This is also true culturally. Many Kurds, who have been educated or lived in Tehran, Tabriz, Baghdad, Mosul, Ankara and Istanbul, feel they belong to a wider world than that of Kurdistan.

Given such a framework, but also the unjust circumstances in which the Kurdish people live, what action can the international community take? The crisis of 1991 demonstrates that the question of Kurdistan will not disappear, and will remain a thorn in the side of regional stability for the foreseeable future.

In the cases of both Iraq and Turkey, it is increasingly difficult for the international community to ignore the growing problem. Turkey's application to join the European Community has been postponed indefinitely, with state treatment of its Kurdish minority being cited as evidence of Turkey's current unsuitability for admission. As in the case of refugees, United Nations Security Council Resolution (UNSCR) 688, relating to the establishment of a Kurdish 'safe haven' in Iraq, sets the precedent of international intervention even inside state borders in order to protect threatened groups. This principle must be widened. The United Nations must involve itself in the fate of the Kurdish people.

Inevitably the governments of the region will see such interest in the well-being of the Kurds as an unwonted interference in their internal affairs. It is important therefore that they should be persuaded by the United Nations of the latter's sincerity to guarantee and uphold their sovereignty and international boundaries, contingent on reasonable treatment of their Kurds in conformity with international law. Furthermore, the United Nations should make it clear to the Kurdish leaderships in the respective countries that any deal struck which affords the Kurds a reasonable say in the running of their own affairs and in cultural self-expression must include Kurdish recognition of state legitimacy. Minorities have duties as well as rights.

To discuss such possibilities may seem unrealistic, but they are a good deal less unrealistic than they appeared when first mooted in the Minority Rights Group report *The Kurds* in March 1989. UNSCR 688 has set a new benchmark in such matters. There is another important advantage in United Nations involvement. Because of political tensions in the region, no government has been able to resist striking deals with the Kurds of a disagreeable neighbour. The involvement of the United Nations in helping individual governments to reach a compromise with its Kurdish minority could usefully be accompanied by United Nations refereeship not only on internal agreements, but also on cases of external interference.

In short, for both the governments and the Kurds of the region, seeking the assistance of the United Nations involves advantages and disadvantages. The task of those that seek both regional stability and the well-being of all communities in the region lies in persuading these governments that the advantages outweigh the disadvantages. This is a challenge not just for the Kurds but for the international community.

Footnotes

David McDowall writes: My notes have been deliberately kept to a minimum. Throughout this book I have drawn extensively on the books mentioned in the bibliography, and for current events on newspapers and periodicals. I should like to emphasize the value of two books hardly used at all by other writers on the Kurdish question, Edmund Ghareeb's on the Iraqi Kurds, and Martin van Bruinessen's study of Kurdish society. Ghareeb's book is not popular with some Kurds who view it as pro-Ba'th, but its careful and factual analysis is superior to any other account of events in Iraq that I have seen. Van Bruinessen's book is in a class of its own, and I can only ascribe its limited use to the fact that, until 1991 when it was re-issued, it was hard to obtain a copy.

[1] Ghareeb, E., *The Kurdish Question in Iraq*, Syracuse, 1981, p.2.
[2] This splendid phrase is not my own; it comes from that great classic on Middle East civilization, Carleton Coon's *Caravan*, New York, 1958.
[3] van Bruinessen, M.M., *Agha, Sheikh and State*, Utrecht University, 1978, p.2.
[4] *Ibid*, p.10.
[5] See for example the maps in Vanly, Ismet Cheriff, *Le Kurd Irakien entite nationale*, Neuchâtel, 1970; and that illustrating Kurdish claims at the Peace Conference 1919 in Nikitine, B., *Les Kurdes, étude sociologique et historique*, Paris, 1956.
[6] Foreign Office, *Armenia and Kurdistan*, May 1919, p.3.
[7] Many Arab families claim almost certainly spurious lineage from the Prophet, whilst most families traditionally belonged to the two parties of north and south Arabia, the Qays and Yamani, though few could indicate their real relationship to these parties with any certainty.
[8] Soane, E.B., *To Mesopotamia and Kurdistan in Disguise*, London, 1912, p.178.
[9] I chose to rely on van Bruinessen, *op cit*, pp.20-22 for guidance, because of his careful attempt at an objective estimate for 1975. I have tried to

update the figures based on the same percentages he used then: in the case of the Iraqi Kurds it is assumed that the Kurds were reliably counted in 1922, and again in 1935 when they constituted approximately 23% of the population. In the case of Iran, the assessment is based on religion, where 10% of the population is Sunni Muslim, of which 1% or so are non-Kurd, and this is offset by the Shi'i Kurds living around Kermanshah. The figure for Turkey is based on van Bruinessen's careful scrutiny of the 1970 census results by sub-province. The unreliability implicit in all these assumptions needs no elaboration, but *faute de mieux* they offer the statistics I have been given. For comparison a recent book to appear on the Kurds, More, C., *Les Kurdes aujourd'hui, mouvement nationale et partis politiques*, Edition Harmattan, Paris, 1984, gives the following Kurdish population percentages: Turkey 24%; Iran 16%; Iraq 27%; Syria 9%; giving a numerical total currently of 20.1 million.

[10] Space does not permit an examination of Yazidi beliefs here, but those interested should consult *The Shorter Encyclopaedia of Islam*, Leiden and London, 1961, 'Yazidi' pp.641-44; Lescot, R., *Enquéte sur les Yezidis*, Librairie du Liban, Beirut, 1975 (reprint of 1938 edition); Drower, E.S., *Peacock Angel*, John Murray, London, 1941; and Layard, A.H., *Nineveh and its Remains*, John Murray, London, 1850. Layard knew several of the Yazidis of Shaikhan and gives a valuable insight into the Yazidi community under persecution by Kurds in the mid-19th Century; Soane, *op cit*, pp.100-103.

[11] This section is based on van Bruinessen's outstanding work, and on the studies by Edmund Leach and Frederick Barth of Kurdish villages in the 1930s and 1940s, summarized in Coon, *Caravan*, pp.298-304, and in Kinnane, *The Kurds and Kurdistan*, London, 1964, pp.10-15. See also Soane, op cit, and Sykes, M., *The Caliph's Last Heritage*, Macmillan, London, 1915, pp.553-588.

[12] Water is the most frequent source of quarrels; during the irrigation season the commonest injuries treated in rural hospitals of west Iran are cranial ones.

[13] Coon, *op cit*, p.304.

[14] Fraser, J.B., *Mesopotamia and Assyria*, Edinburgh, 1842, p.310.

[15] The Naqshabandis had originally been encouraged by the Ottomans as a counter-weight to Baban friendliness with Persia. A popular Sunni brotherhood in the Baban capital of Sulaymaniya, strongly connected with orthodoxy in Baghdad, would make an alliance with Shi'i Persia dangerous locally for the Babans. As a result, when Persia invaded in 1818 the Babans stayed at home. Possibly alarmed at wild Naqshabandi practices, and the implicit threat to Sunni orthodoxy in the Empire, the Ottomans thereafter dropped the Naqshabandi connection, More, *op cit*, p.51.

[16]   Kinnane, D., *The Kurds and Kurdistan*, OUP, London, 1964, p.24.

[17]   The Russians had tried to bring Kurds in on their own side in wars with Turkey in 1829 and 1853-55, and even tried to raise a regiment of Kurds under Russian officers. In 1877 when the Turks were fighting the Russians around Erzerum and Van, the sons of Badr Khan rose in rebellion in Hakkari, Badinan and Buhtan.

[18]   Kendal in Chaliand, C., *People without a Country*, p.43 explains how the determination of the border between Armenian and Kurdish areas had already been made subject to President Wilson's decision, as referee. Amongst those areas already provisionally allocated to the Armenian state were several where it could be argued that a Kurdish majority existed.

[19]   First adumbrated in the Amasya Protocol, and repeated in the National Pact of 1920, see Kendal in Chaliand, *op cit*, p.56.

[20]   Quoted by Kendal in Chaliand, *op cit*, p.65.

[21]   *Milliyet* No 1655, 16/9/30, quoted by Kendal in Chaliand, *op cit*, p.66.

[22]   *Kurdistan News and Comment*, No 5, March 1981, p.21.

[23]   Ghareeb, *op cit*, p.10

[24]   van Bruinessen, 'Between guerrilla war and political murder: The Workers' Party of Kurdistan,' *Middle East Report*, No 153, July-August 1988, p.42.

[25]   Gunter, M., *The Kurds in Turkey*, Boulder, 1990, p.77.

[26]   *Turkey Briefing*, Vol 1, No 2, March 1987.

[27]   *Turkey Briefing*, Vol 1, No 4, July 1987.

[28]   *Turkey Briefing*, Vol 1, No 5, September 1987.

[29]   Gunter, *The Kurds in Turkey*, p.83.

[30]   *Cumhuriyet*, 12/2/86, quoted by van Bruinessen in *Middle East Report*, *op cit*.

[31]   Amnesty International, *Turkey Briefing*, November 1988 reports: 'The most severe allegations of torture have come from south and south-eastern Turkey, where the Kurdish population is concentrated. Most deaths in custody as a result of torture are reported in these regions... In their search for members and supporters of the guerrilla groups, the security forces have rounded up entire villages and beaten them. Often young male inhabitants are beaten up and sometimes taken to the nearest police station and ill-treated for several days. But women and old men are also reported to have been the target of humiliating treatment...' See also *Turkey: Brutal and Systematic Abuse of Human Rights*, January 1989.

[32]   See, for example, *The Independent*, 21/7/89.

[33]   For evidence, see Helsinki Watch, *Destroying Ethnic Identity*, September 1990, pp.19-23.

[34]   *Turkey Briefing*, Vol 3, No 5, September 1989.

[35] The largest clash to date had occurred on 1 April 1988, in vhich 20 PKK guerrillas were reportedly killed, *Turkey Briefing*, Vol 2, Nc 3, July 1988.

[36] *Ibid.*

[37] Gunter, *op cit*, p.88.

[38] *Turkey Briefing*, Vol 2, No 2, March 1988.

[39] *Turkey Briefing*, Vol 2, No 4, see also Gunter, op cit, p.88.

[40] *Turkey Briefing*, Vol 2, No 2, March 1988, and Vol 2, No 6, November 1988.

[41] *Turkey Briefing*, Vol 3, No 1, January 1989.

[42] See for example, *The Guardian*, 21/1/88.

[43] This was particularly important as the 25 September referendum he had called to obtain the electorate's consent to a constitutional amendment to bring forward the local elections in advance of the fixed five-year term. Özal threatened to resign if there was a significant vote against him. He did not obtain the electorate's assent but decided the vote against him had not been significant, *Turkey Briefing*, Vol 2, No 5.

[44] Turkey is a signatory of the 1951 Convention on Refugees, which refers only to those affected by events in Europe prior to 1 January 1951. The protocol of 1967 amended the remit of the Convention so that its provisions were no longer limited by time or space; see *The Refugee Dilemma*, (MRG Report); but Turkey did not accede to the Protocol. It has consequently been unable, legally, to consider the Kurds as refugees. Thus it allowed UNHCR access to the Kurdish camps, it being understood that the Kurds, while being 'persons of interest to UNHCR' were not refugees.

[45] *The Independent*, 24/1/89.

[46] See reports in *The Independent*, 31/1/89 and 7/6/89.

[47] *Turkey Briefing*, Vol 3, No 6, November 1989.

[48] *Turkey Briefing*, Vol 4, No 2, April 1990.

[49] *Turkey Briefing*, vol 4 No 2.

[50] Quoted from the translation in *Turkey Briefing*, Vol 4, No 3, June 1990; see also for a discussion of Kararname 413, Helsinki Watch, *Destroying Ethnic Identity*, September 1990.

[51] In December it was renumbered yet again, becoming Kararname 430, in order to pre-empt the Constitutional Court, see *Turkey Briefing*, Vol 5, No 1, February 1991.

[52] See examples quoted by Helsinki Watch, *Destroying Ethnic Identity*, September 1990, p.24.

[53] *Turkey Briefing*, Vol 5, No 2, April 1991.

[54] Which only seven months earlier, in July 1990, had published its own policy document on the Kurdish region calling for cultural rights.

[55] For the full text see Helsinki Watch, 'Turkey: new Restrictive Anti-Terror Law', 10/6/91.

[56] McDowall, D., Comment in *Turkey Briefing*, Vol 5, No 1, February 1991.

[57] *Ibid.*

[58] Oral information from the Diyarbekir Human Rights Association, October 1990.

[59] Mahmut Baksi, 'The immigrant experience in Sweden', *MERIP Report*, May 1984, p.19.

[60] Kurds and Turks disagree over the number of Alevis. Some Turks maintain that there are at least 18 million Alevis to be found all over Turkey (and as far west as Albania and Yugoslavia). This definition seems to embrace many adherents of the Sufi or dervish mystical orders with Shi'ite leanings, particularly the Bektashi Order. This paper accepts the usual Kurdish definition which confines the definition to people known as Alevis in the region roughly bounded by the towns of Kirshehir – Sivas – Erzerum – Elazig – Gaziantep – Marash – Kayseri.

[61] For the early history and beliefs of the Kizilbash, see Matti Moosa, *Extremist Shi'ites: The Ghulat Sects*, Syracuse University Press, 1988, particularly chapters 3, 4, 5, and 38.

[62] Hastings, J., (Ed) *Encyclopaedia of Religion and Ethics*, Edinburgh, 1926, Vol vii, p.744.

[63] A very useful summary on the Kurdish Alevis is Bumke, P., 'The Kurdish Alevis – boundaries and perceptions' in Alford Andrews, P., (Ed), *Ethnic Groups in the Republic of Turkey*, Wiesbaden, 1989, pp.511-518.

[64] Quoted from unsworn affidavits made by asylum-seekers.

[65] *Middle East Report*, No 153, July-August 1988

[66] *Unilever Monitor*, No 4, December-February 1988.

[67] Oral information from Dr Alexander Sternberg-Spohr, Kurdish expert at Gesellschaft fur Bedrohte Völker, Gottingen, Germany.

[68] *Ibid.*

[69] See for an example *The Observer*, 25/6/89.

[70] Quoted from affidavit made by an asylum-seeker.

[71] See the fascinating account by van Bruinessen, 'Kurdish Tribes and Simko's Revolt' in Tapper, R., (Ed), *The Conflict of Tribe and State in Iran and Afghanistan*, Croom Helm, London, 1983, pp.364-396.

[72] Roosevelt in Chaliand, *op cit*, p.139. (These were Qaranei Agha of the Mamesh, Amr Khan Sharifi of the Shikak, and Amir Asad of the Dehbokri).

[73] Entessar, N., 'The Kurds in Post Revolutionary Iran and Iraq', *Third World Quarterly*, 9(4) October 1984, p.923; see also for a fascinating account of the Jaf and Ardelan tribes at the turn of the century, Soane, *op cit.*

[74] *MERIP Report*, March 1983, pp.9-10.

[75] *The Independent*, August 1989.

[76] Indispensable reading on the early Mandate period are Toynbee, A.J., *A*

Survey of International Affairs 1925, OUP, London, 1927; Wilson, Sir A., *Mesopotamia 1917-1920, a Clash of Loyalties*, OUP, London, 1931; Sluglett, P., *Britain in Iraq 1914-1932*, St Antony's College, Oxford, 1976.

77 Toynbee, *op cit*, p.479 quoting the League Commission Report, p.57.

78 *Ibid*.

79 Shaikh Mahmud himself made no attempt to present himself or his claims to the League Commission investigating Turkish and Anglo-Iraqi claims concerning the Mosul vilayet, even though its deliberations directly affected a large part of Kurdistan, Kinnane, *op cit*, p.39.

80 Sluglett, *op cit*, p.183.

81 Strictly speaking it was his elder brother, Ahmad, who succeeded Shaikh Mahmud but he retired from active involvement in 1936.

82 Space does not permit discussion of the fate of the Assyrian Christians except to say that they also were victims of the collapse of the old order and the creation of nation-states in the region. Hoping for assistance from Christian countries, notably Russia and Britain, they rebelled against the Turks in their traditional areas, around Hakkari, Tur Abdin and also against the Iranians in Urmiya. The remnants that survived war and massacre ended up under British protection in Iraq (where they suffered another major massacre in 1933).

83 Essential reading for this period is Ghareeb, *op cit*, and Sa'ad Jawad, *Iraq and the Kurdish Question 1958-1970*, Ithaca, London, 1981.

84 Ghareeb, *op cit*, p.38.

85 *Ibid*, p.37.

86 *Ibid*, p.41.

87 *Ibid*, p.65: this included a form of self-administration allowing Kurds to participate in running their own educational, economic and social affairs. It retained, however, governmental control over all key or sensitive issues.

88 Ghareeb, *op cit*, p.87; for full text see previous MRG Report, The Kurds, 1975 (o/p) p.21.

89 Barzani in Ghareeb, *op cit*, p.89.

90 Ghareeb, *op cit*, p.115.

91 *Ibid*, p.153.

92 *Ibid*, p.155.

93 For full text see *The Kurds*, MRG Report, 1975 (o/p) p.22. Although KDP had agreed earlier to its use, in 1971, it subsequently challenged the validity of an out-of-date census. Since then there had been mutual accusations of trying to change the demographic balance in sensitive areas. In the Kurdish view only 60% of the Kurdish area was included in the autonomous region. Arbil was designated as the administrative centre.

94 Latham, A., *What Kissinger was Afraid of in the Pike Papers*, New York,

October 1974, p.68, in Ghareeb, *op cit*, p.159.

[95] Also confirmed by Americans, *ibid*.

[96] For complete text see *The Kurds*, MRG Report, 1985 (o/p) p.24.

[97] Ghareeb, *op cit*, p.183.

[98] These included: (1) return of up to 200,000 Kurds resettled in south Iraq: agreed to but not implemented; (2) establishment of democratic professional organizations: agreed to but not implemented; (3) disagreement over the amnesty of political prisoners. PUK insisted on the release of all Kurdish political prisoners, whilst this was refused except in the case of PUK members. According to PUK the government executed a large number of these detainees; (4) re-establishment of the University of Sulaymaniya and of cultural, educational and media activities in Kurdish: largely not implemented.

[99] These groups were the KDP, PUK, the Iraqi Kurdistan Socialist Party, the Iraqi Kurdistan People's Democratic Party and the Kurdish Socialist Party (PASOK).

[100] See *Middle East International*, No 314, 5/12/87.

[101] See press statement of PUK, dated 17/3/87 and Amnesty International statement of 25/2/87. Amnesty International was neither allowed to investigate nor able to obtain information from the authorities concerning the fate of those minors they had arrested in September 1985.

[102] Claim made by Jalal Talabani, 9/3/88.

[103] *Middle East International*, No 333, 9/9/88.

[104] *Ibid*.

[105] See PUK communique of 19/10/88.

[106] Private interview, 9/2/90.

[107] It should be noted that Talabani himself denied seeking a meeting, and stated that he was merely obliging an intermediary since he happened to be in Washington at the time.

[108] *The Independent*, 20/9/90.

[109] Other leading parties were the Council of Islamic Revolution (Shi'i), Islamic Da'wa Party, the Iraqi Communist Party, the Arab National Movement, the Ba'th Party (opposition).

[110] It was able to meet British Foreign Office officials, in January where it was listened to sympathetically, but Britain was unable to persuade the United States to take it seriously.

[111] *The Independent*, 3/4/91.

[112] See for example *The Observer*, 14/4/91.

[113] *The Observer*, 28/4/91.

[114] *The Independent*, 1/4/91.

[115] See for example *The Independent*, 30/5/91.

[116] For this section I have drawn primarily on the following: Mustafa Nazdar,

'The Kurds in Syria', in Chaliand, *op cit*; Petran, T., *Syria*, Benn, London, 1972; Longrigg, S.H., *Syria and Lebanon under the French Mandate*, OUP, London, 1947; Seale, P., *The Struggle for Syria*, OUP, London, 1965; van Dam, N., *The Struggle for Power in Syria*, Croom Helm, London, 1979.

[117] The famous *Krak des Chevaliers*, known in Arabic as the Castle of the Kurds (*Husn al Akrad*), is one such site. Likewise, the Salhiyya quarter of Damascus has had a strong Kurdish character since the time of Saladin in the 12th Century, and is probably connected to a Kurdish military colony.

[118] van Dam, *op cit*, p.44; Seale, *op cit*, p.160.

[119] For example, Kurds allege that in 1988 or 1989 200 Kurdish students were expelled from educational institutes.

[120] This section borrows heavily from Kendal in Chaliand, *op cit*, pp.220-228.

[121] Chaliand, *op cit*, p.227.

[122] Nadirov, N., 'Position of the Kurds in USSR', paper presented to the Kurdish Symposium, Pantheion University, Athens, 6/6/91, p.6.

[123] Heyderi, J., 'The Kurds of the USSR', paper presented to the Symposium on Kurdish Rights, Stockholm, March 1991, p.6. Another 2000 Kurds have fled from Uzbekistan. In Kirgizhia Kurds have also been told to quit.

[124] *Ibid*.

[125] Nadirov, N., *op cit*, p.4.

[126] *Ibid*.

[127] Summary extract from Vanly, I.C., *Kurdistan und die Kurden*, The Kurds in USSR. See also Nadirov, *op cit*, p.4.

[128] Most of this evidence comes from Physicians for Human Rights statement of 22/10/88, and the Senate Foreign Relations Committee Report of September 1988.

[129] *New York Times*, 15/9/88, cited in Senate Foreign Relations Committee Report, p.30.

[130] Roberts, G., *Winds of Death*, a film shown on *Dispatches*, Channel 4, 23/11/88.

[131] *The Times*, 8/6/88.

[132] It was reluctant to use the word 'evidence' since its evidence had apparently been obtained by means of covert surveillance which it did not want to reveal.

[133] In the year 1987/88 this had amounted to £175 million. For 1988/89 it was increased to £340 million.

[134] *The Independent*, 23/11/88.

Select Bibliography

ARFA, Hassan, *The Kurds, An Historical and Political Study*, OUP, London, 1966.

BOIS, Thomas, *The Kurds*, Khayats, Beirut, 1965.

BRUINESSEN, Martin van, *Agha, Shaikh and State*, Utrecht University, 1978 (reissued by Zed Books, London, 1991.

CARDRI, *Saddam's Iraq, Revolution or Reaction?*, Zed Books, London, 1989.

CHALIAND, Gérard, *People without a Country*, Zed Books, London, 1980. (Also available in French, *Les Kurdes et Kurdistan*, Petite Collection Maspero, Paris, 1978.)

EAGLETON, William, *The Kurdish Republic of 1946*, OUP, London, 1963.

EDMONDS, C.J., *Kurds, Turks and Arabs*, London, 1957.

ENCYCLOPAEDIA OF ISLAM, E.J. Brill, Leiden, 1981, Vol 5, Fasc-85-86, 'Kurds'.

FAROUK-SLUGLETT, Marion, and SLUGLETT, Peter, *Iraq Since 1958, from Revolution to Dictatorship*, KPI, London, 1987 and I.B. Tauris (paperback edition), 1990.

GHASSEMLOU, Abdul Rahman, *The Kurds and Kurdistan*, London and Prague, 1965.

GUNTER, Michael, *The Kurds in Turkey*, Boulder, Colorado, 1990.

HELSINKI WATCH, *Destroying Ethnic Identity: The Kurds in Turkey*, Washington, March 1980, update September 1990.

JAWAD, Sa'ad, *Iraq and the Kurdish Question*, 1958-70, Ithaca, London, 1981.

KINNANE, Derk, *The Kurds and Kurdistan*, OUP, London, 1964.

KUTSCHERA, Chris, *Le mouvement national kurde*, Flammarion, Paris, 1979.

MIDDLE EAST WATCH, *Human Rights in Iraq*, February 1990.

MORE, Christiane, *Les Kurdes aujourd'hui, mouvement nationale et partis politiques*, Edition Harmattan, Paris, 1984.

NIKITINE, Basile, *Les Kurdes, étude sociologique et historique*, Paris, 1956.

OLSON, Robert, *The Emergence of Kurdish Nationalism and the Sheikh Said Rebellion, 1880-1925*, Austin, Texas, 1989.

ROBINS, Philip, *Turkey and the Middle East*, Pinter, London, 1991.

SHARAF AL DIN KHAN of Bitlis: *Sharafnameh or Les fastes de la nation kurde*, translated by F. Charmoy, St. Petersburg, 1868-76, a 16th Century account of the Kurdish people and their chiefs.

SOANE, E.B, *To Mesopotamia and Kurdistan in Disguise*, London, 1912.

INDEX

About Minority Rights Group Reports

The Minority Rights Group began publishing in 1970. Over two decades and ninety titles later, MRG's series of reports are widely recognized internationally as authoritative, accurate and objective documents on the rights of minorities worldwide.

Over the years, subscribers to the series have received a wealth of unique material on ethnic, religious, linguistic and social minorities. The reports are seen as an important reference by researchers, students, campaigners and provide readers all over the world with valuable background data on many current affairs issues.

Around six reports are published every year. Each title, expertly researched and written, is approximately 30 pages and 20,000 words long and covers a specific minority issue.

Recent titles in our report series include:

Europe
Romania's Ethnic Hungarians
Refugees in Europe

Middle East
Beduin of the Negev
The Kurds

General
Language, Literacy and Minorities

Americas
Maya of Guatemala

Africa
The Sahel
Somalia

Southern Oceans
Maori of Aotearoa-New Zealand
The Pacific: Nuclear Testing and Minorities

Asia
Afghanistan
Bangladesh

If you have found this book informative and stimulating, and would like to learn more about minority issues, please do subscribe to our

report series. It is only with the help of our supporters that we are
to pursue our aims and objectives – to secure justice for disadvant
groups around the world.

We currently offer a reduced annual rate for individual subscribers –
please ring our Subscription Desk on 071 978 9498 for details. Payment
can be easily made by MasterCard or Visa over the telephone or by
post.

All enquiries to: Sales Department
                    The Minority Rights Group
                    379 Brixton Road
                    London
                    SW9 7DE
                    United Kingdom.

Customers in North America wishing to purchase copies of our reports
should contact:
                    Cultural Survival
                    53 Church Street
                    Cambridge
                    MA 02138
                    USA